BYRON

THE COOKBOOK

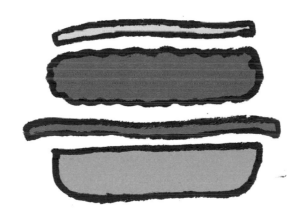

TOM BYNG & FRED SMITH

BYRON

THE COOKBOOK

quadrille

CONTENTS

INTRODUCTION

I owe my life in hamburgers to a single late-night grill. I was 21 and at university in America when my friends and I stumbled on the Silver Top, a diner in Providence, Rhode Island. It was 1a.m. and we'd been drinking, an activity they take pretty seriously in that part of the East Coast. The burger, when it came, didn't look that special. But when I tasted it, everything came together in a way that the drab, grey patties I'd eaten back home never had. The beef was succulent, the bun was perfectly squishy and the cheese was soft and comforting. We ate our burgers silently with hot, salty fries and, from then on, burgers at the Silver Top became a regular part of my student life.

I returned home from the States with only a rough idea of what to do with my life. After a short spell in advertising I fell into restaurants, owning and running a couple in London's Notting Hill when the area was much less trendy than it is today.

By 2006, the rents had become unaffordable. I needed a new challenge – and I remembered the Silver Top. It almost surprises me to think about it today, but burgers in Britain were still pretty dreadful back then. Too many restaurants served mediocre, overcooked minced beef in dry buns with a splat of cheese. Then, of course, there were the huge chains. To me, these lacked soul and were too obviously about labs and logistics. I wanted to make proper burgers the way I remembered them from the misspent nights of my American youth.

There was a clear idea from the start. We would keep things simple: a classic burger, a cheeseburger, a chicken burger and a veggie burger. Three salads, homemade fries and sizzling onion rings would complement the star. The beef would be of high quality and sourced carefully, the buns made fresh each day. Byron, of course, was a great English poet; I liked the contrast between his British name and our American food. We looked in the dictionary and discovered that "byron" comes from the Old English word for "cowshed". So it almost seemed like fate.

We found a site at the unfashionable end of Kensington High Street and launched in

December 2007. We were busy from the start, and I think I know why. Made with honesty and good ingredients, and above all kept simple, the hamburger is a pleasure – and not necessarily a guilty one.

Then, in 2012, I heard about a chef who was making some of the best burgers in London from a small pub kitchen. I went to The Admiral Codrington one night, tried his burger and said to myself: this is far too good. Fred Smith and I met for several cups of coffee over the following weeks, eventually agreeing to collaborate on a special Byron burger for the Royal Jubilee that summer. We cheekily named it The Chilli Queen, it was a huge success, and soon Fred came to work with us full time.

Since then, he and I have eaten dozens – possibly hundreds – of burgers across the US: in Miami, Dallas, Kentucky, Los Angeles, San Francisco, San Diego and New York. We've travelled to other countries on similar adventures, even going to Paris to taste the best burgers the French can make. (They are very good, if you were wondering – see page 26.) We think we know how to make a good burger – perhaps one of the best. This book is our attempt to share our knowledge and experience with you.

Fred will explain how to keep a burger juicy and make your own buns and sauces; he will outline the best techniques for the BBQ as well as the hob if barbecuing isn't an option. He'll reveal the best cuts of beef, how to blitz the perfect milkshake and how to make fries crisp outside and fluffy within. We keep our menus simple at Byron, but Fred and I have also included diner dishes that we've loved on our travels. Our goal has been to design doable recipes that lift the spirits and warm the soul.

Since Byron was born, the British burger scene has transformed beyond recognition. The average hamburger you find in your local pub or restaurant tastes incomparably better than it used to. Chefs use better beef, cook ingredients more carefully and, only rarely these days, bring out the ciabatta. I'm proud that Byron has played a role in these changes, and my hope is that this book will bring the joy of my first Silver Top experience to burger-lovers everywhere.

– *Tom Byng*

HAMBURGERS

Our classic hamburger patty hasn't changed since we opened the first restaurant. Fred has tried a few times to tweak it by varying the cuts and proportions, but nothing seems to improve it. I remember the 7.30a.m. tastings, the endless back-and-forths with the butcher, and the final, happy realisation that we had hit on something good. This chapter explains how to make the best hamburgers you could hope to, and gives advice on how to cook them.

quintessential beef dishes: don't skimp on the main ingredient. Barbecues and frying pans give you equally good – but different – results. When fat and juices drip onto hot charcoal, they sizzle, create smoke and help to season the meat. A cast-iron pan, by contrast, delivers a better caramelised surface to a burger. Ultimately, which method you choose will depend on season and circumstance, but both will be delicious.

IT GOES WITHOUT SAYING THAT THE BEEF IS THE MOST IMPORTANT THING. WE USE A MIXTURE OF CHUCK, SKIRT, BRISKET AND RIB FAT IN THE RESTAURANTS, FOR THEIR UNBEATABLE COMBINATION OF TEXTURE AND FLAVOUR.

If you're cooking for large numbers of people then you might want to use the same blend of cuts as we do. But you'll get fantastic results by just using freshly minced chuck steak, which comes from the animal's forequarter. This is about 20% fat, which will keep the patty succulent and tender, as well as lending it a beefy, savoury taste.

The fresher you can get your mince, the better. As a minimum, this means asking your butcher to grind the beef for you. Ideally, you'll mince it at home the same day or, at most, the day before you want to cook it. Avoid packets of mince from supermarket chiller cabinets. These are likely to be several days old; ground beef left for ages tends to "set" and clag together. You also won't know what parts of the beast have been used, and the meat may have been sealed with gases to keep it "fresh". The hamburger is one of the

Most shop-bought buns can't shake a stick at the ones you make at home. A proper hamburger bun is sturdy and doesn't collapse when it soaks up the juices. You don't exactly want a crust – remember the grim Ciabatta Days of the 1990s? – but you do need something that has a little bit of chew and isn't too "cakey". Anything made with butter is good. If you feel that life is too short to make your own, then source ready-made burger buns that are reassuringly rich and buttery.

We haven't held back on the recipes in this chapter. We wanted to show you the incredible versatility of the hamburger – how different meats and flavours can create dramatically varying experiences. But, irrespective of the accompaniments and changes, each of these hamburgers – all those made with beef, at least – comes back to the unbeatable patty I hit upon in Byron's first kitchen.

BEEF

GRINDING THE MEAT

Always grind the meat on the day you intend to use it. Ask your butcher for chuck steak, ground twice through a 4–6mm plate. To mince beef at home, cut the chuck steak into 1cm cubes and place in the freezer for 15–20 minutes to make sure it is very cold. You can also put the mincer in the freezer. Good mincing attachments are available for mixers. A small, stand-alone electric mincer is great; an old-school hand mincer will do.

FORMING THE PATTIES

Divide the mince into 180g portions and roll by hand into balls. Place onto squares of greaseproof paper. If shaping by hand, take one portion between your palms. Cup the edges of the mince with one hand and push with the other. Turn your hands as you press them together and shape the mince into an even patty about 12cm wide and 1.5cm thick.

If using a burger press, buy one that will give you a 11–12cm wide burger; they are easy to find online. Put one 180g ball of mince between two sheets of greaseproof paper (usually provided with the burger press) and follow the instructions.

CHILLING

Store the patties separated by squares of greaseproof paper. Wrap and refrigerate for at least 1 hour before cooking.

CHOOSING BURGER BUNS

The best buns are homemade – see page 58 for my recipe. Alternatively, find a local baker who bakes burger buns. In the supermarket, always look for an "enriched" dough – something with a little butter and some egg in the recipe. Try giving shop-bought buns a gentle squeeze: they should give a little, and not crack on the surface.

HAMBURGERS ON A BBQ

PREPARATION

Buy a BBQ with a lid. Charcoal is preferable to gas.
Get the temperature right: you want it hot but without flames. Slow-burning embers are best, and the BBQ is ready once the charcoal is white around the edges. When you add the meat, the fat will drip down and can create flames, so be careful.

GRILLING

Ideally salt one side of the patty just before it goes on the grill and then season the other side while cooking. Do not crowd the cooking space: you should only use about 50% of the grill surface, with enough room to turn the patties.
The patty should sizzle as soon as it touches the grill. If it doesn't, leave the BBQ to heat up further.
A crowded BBQ will lose all its heat, leaving the meat to sweat, fail to brown properly and stick.

To toast the burger buns, place them, cut-side down, towards the edge of the BBQ, where it is cooler. Toast them lightly.
Turn the patty three times in total: about once every minute. As fat drips, it can create flames. If this does happen you should move the patty to a different part of the grill. When you start to see little drops of pink juice forming on the patty's surface, cook for a further minute and serve for a pink and juicy hamburger.

CHEESE

After the final turn of the patty, lay the cheese on top.
Close the BBQ lid to melt the cheese.

TOOLS

I like a "flipper", as it will help if there is any sticking. Make sure to buy a flameproof one with a long handle. Some people like tongs. To own both is even better.

Don't use a fork or anything sharp, as you will pierce the meat and lose the juices.
If your BBQ doesn't have a lid, use a cloche (an upturned metal mixing bowl).

HAMBURGERS IN THE KITCHEN

PREPARATION

A heavy, non-stick frying pan is best. At home I use a cast-iron frying pan, as it holds heat well. Heat the pan for at least 4–5 minutes over a medium–high heat (slightly less on an induction hob). To tell if the pan is hot enough, add a couple of drops of water to the pan: if they evaporate immediately or form into little balls that scatter across the pan's surface then you're at the right temperature. If they don't, keep heating the pan until they do. Open windows or turn on the extractor fan if necessary. It is worth getting the pan super-hot.

COOKING

Season the patties generously with fine sea salt and a couple of grinds of black pepper on both sides, just before adding to the pan. Place the patty in the pan and gently push the centre down as it hits the pan to prevent curling and maximise caramelisation.

Don't overcrowd the pan – cook in batches and make sure the burgers do not touch. Turn the patty three times in total: once every minute or so. When you start to see little drops of pink juice forming on the surface, cook for a further minute and then serve immediately for a pink and juicy hamburger.

TOASTING

Toast the cut sides of the buns either under a preheated grill or face down in a large, dry frying pan over a medium–high heat. Remove once golden.

Buns with a high butter content will take about 2 minutes in a dry frying pan or 30 seconds under a grill. Others containing no butter can take up to 4 minutes in a frying pan or 1 minute under a grill.

CHEESE

Line a small oven tray with foil and arrange the cooked burgers, topped with the cheese, on top. Keep a close eye on the cheese – it will melt faster than you expect.

TOOLS

A fish slice or "flipper" is the easiest tool for turning burgers. If you don't have a grill to melt the cheese then you can use a cloche (an upturned metal mixing bowl) or a large raised saucepan lid to cover the patty in the pan, which will create enough heat to melt the cheese.

CLASSIC

A hamburger for people who relish the simple things. This, above all others,
has stood the test of time – hence its name.

MAKES 4

INGREDIENTS

4 X 180g HAMBURGERS (SEE PAGE 14)

4 BUNS, HALVED

100g MAYONNAISE

4 LEAVES OF LETTUCE, SUCH AS ESCAROLE, LOLLO VERDE
OR CURLY LEAF GREEN LETTUCE

½ BEEF TOMATO, CUT INTO 5mm THICK SLICES

1 SMALL RED ONION, PEELED AND CUT INTO
2mm THICK RINGS

4 GHERKIN SPEARS

METHOD

1. Cook the hamburgers to your liking following the instructions on pages 16–17.

2. Meanwhile, toast or grill the cut sides of the buns.

3. Spread the mayonnaise evenly over the top halves of the buns.

4. Place one lettuce leaf on top of the mayonnaise, then add a slice of tomato. Separate the onion into rings and place 5 of these on top of the tomato.

5. Once the hamburgers are cooked, carefully place them onto the bottom halves of the buns.

6. Holding on to the lettuce, tomato and onion rings, bring the 2 halves together.

7. Serve with a gherkin spear on the side.

CHEESE

People around the world love the flavour and texture that melted cheese brings
to a hamburger – so it's small wonder this is our biggest seller in the restaurants.
We urge you to try this with Fred's Homemade Cheese Slices (see page 94).

MAKES 4

INGREDIENTS

4 X 180g HAMBURGERS (SEE PAGE 14)

4 BUNS, HALVED

100g MAYONNAISE

4 LEAVES OF LETTUCE, SUCH AS ESCAROLE,
LOLLO VERDE OR CURLY LEAF GREEN LETTUCE

½ BEEF TOMATO, CUT INTO 5mm THICK SLICES

1 SMALL RED ONION, PEELED AND CUT INTO
2mm THICK RINGS

4 SLICES OF YOUR CHOSEN CHEESE, ROUGHLY THE
SAME SIZE AS THE HAMBURGERS

4 GHERKIN SPEARS

METHOD

1. Preheat the grill to high.

2. Cook the hamburgers to your liking following
the instructions on pages 16–17.

3. Meanwhile, toast or grill the cut sides of
the buns.

4. Spread the mayonnaise evenly over the top
halves of the buns.

5. Place one lettuce leaf on top of the
mayonnaise, then add a slice of tomato.
Separate the onion into rings and place 5
of these on top of the tomato.

6. Once the hamburgers are cooked, transfer
them to a small oven tray lined with foil. Top
each hamburger with a slice of cheese. Place
under the hot grill on the highest shelf. Watch
carefully and remove the tray from under the
grill as soon as the cheese has melted. If using
a BBQ, follow the instructions for melting
cheese on page 16.

7. Carefully place the hamburgers onto the
bottom halves of the buns and bring the
2 halves together.

8. Serve with a gherkin spear on the side.

BYRON

Our signature hamburger:
a classic combination of beef, melted Cheddar and dry-cured bacon with a dollop of our famous sauce.

MAKES 4

INGREDIENTS

4 X 180G HAMBURGERS (SEE PAGE 14)

4 BUNS, HALVED

100G BYRON SAUCE (SEE PAGE 88)

¼ ICEBERG LETTUCE, LEAVES FINELY SHREDDED

½ BEEF TOMATO, CUT INTO 5MM THICK SLICES

1 SMALL RED ONION, PEELED AND CUT INTO 2MM THICK RINGS

4 SLICES OF CHEDDAR CHEESE, ROUGHLY THE SAME SIZE AS THE HAMBURGERS

8 SLICES OF CRISPY SMOKED STREAKY BACON (SEE PAGE 94)

4 GHERKIN SPEARS

METHOD

1. Preheat the grill to high.

2. Cook the hamburgers to your liking following the instructions on page 16–17.

3. Meanwhile, toast or grill the cut sides of the buns.

4. Spread the Byron Sauce evenly over the top halves of the buns.

5. Place the shredded lettuce on the bottom halves of the buns and add a slice of tomato. Place 5 onion rings on top of each tomato.

6. When the hamburgers are cooked, transfer them to a small roasting tray. Top each one with a slice of Cheddar and 2 slices of bacon. Place under the hot grill on the highest shelf. Watch carefully and remove the tray from under the grill as soon as the cheese has melted. If using a BBQ, follow the instructions for melting cheese on page 16.

7. Carefully place the hamburgers onto the bottom halves of the buns and bring the 2 halves together.

8. Serve with a gherkin spear on the side.

CHILLI QUEEN

Fred created this as a special to celebrate the Queen's Golden Jubilee in 2012.
It has plenty of kick and is for strong constitutions only. Its popularity earned it a permanent place
on the Byron menu when we celebrated our fifth birthday.

MAKES 4

INGREDIENTS

1 TSP OLIVE OIL

4 LONG GREEN CHILLIES, ABOUT 80G IN TOTAL, SLICED

4 X 180G HAMBURGERS (SEE PAGE 14)

4 BUNS, HALVED

¼ ICEBERG LETTUCE, FINELY SHREDDED

120G CHIPOTLE MAYO (SEE PAGE 88)

8 SLICES OF AMERICAN CHEESE, ROUGHLY THE SAME SIZE AS THE HAMBURGERS

4 GHERKIN SPEARS

METHOD

1. Preheat the grill to high.

2. Add the olive oil to a small saucepan over a medium heat. Once hot, add the sliced chillies and cook for 2 minutes – they should be only very lightly cooked and still crunchy.

3. Cook the hamburgers to your liking following the instructions on pages 16–17.

4. Meanwhile, toast or grill the cut sides of the buns.

5. Place the shredded lettuce on the bottom halves of the buns.

6. Add a spoonful of the Chipotle Mayo to the top halves of the buns and place another spoonful on top of the shredded lettuce.

7. When the hamburgers are cooked, transfer to a small roasting tray. Top each hamburger with the fried chillies, followed by 2 slices of cheese, making sure the chillies are covered. Place under the hot grill on the highest shelf. Watch carefully and remove the tray from under the grill as soon as the cheese has melted. If using a BBQ, follow the instructions for melting cheese on page 16.

8. Carefully place the hamburgers onto the bottom halves of the buns and bring the 2 halves together.

9. Serve with a gherkin spear on the side.

LE SMOKEY

Fred created this burger following a trip to Paris. We'd heard that Paris was undergoing a burger revolution like London's but, perhaps unfairly, we were expecting a surfeit of Camembert and beef patties invariably cooked "bleu". Au contraire. The influences were undeniably American: "Obama" burgers, tacos, iPad ordering systems and lots of BBQ sauce. We've added other punchy flavours here including chipotle, pancetta and crispy onions. The result is terrific.

MAKES 4

INGREDIENTS

100g BYRON SPICY BBQ SAUCE (SEE PAGE 89)

2 TBSP CHIPOTLE MAYO (SEE PAGE 88)

4 X 180g HAMBURGERS (SEE PAGE 14)

4 BUNS, HALVED

¼ ICEBERG LETTUCE, FINELY SHREDDED

16 GHERKIN SLICES

4 SLICES OF SMOKED CHEDDAR CHEESE, ROUGHLY THE SAME SIZE AS THE HAMBURGERS

12 SLICES OF CRISPY PANCETTA (SEE PAGE 95)

100g SHOP-BOUGHT CRISPY ONION PIECES

4 GHERKIN SPEARS

METHOD

1. Preheat the grill to high.

2. In a small bowl, mix the Byron Spicy BBQ Sauce and Chipotle Mayo to create a smoky BBQ sauce. Set aside.

3. Cook the hamburgers to your liking following the instructions on pages 16–17.

4. Meanwhile, toast or grill the cut sides of the buns.

5. Place the shredded lettuce on the bottom halves of the buns. Top with 4 slices of gherkin.

6. Add a spoonful of the smoky BBQ sauce to both halves of the buns.

7. When the hamburgers are cooked, transfer to a small roasting tray. Top each hamburger with a slice of cheese and 3 slices of Crispy Pancetta. Place under the hot grill on the highest shelf. Watch carefully and remove the tray from under the grill as soon as the cheese has melted. If using a BBQ, follow the instructions for melting cheese on page 16.

8. Carefully place the hamburgers onto the bottom halves of the buns and cover them completely with crispy onion pieces.

9. Bring the 2 halves together and serve with a gherkin spear on the side.

B-REX

Can anything taste as good as the memory of your favourite hamburger as a child? That's the question Fred set out to answer with this burger – our most popular special ever. It evokes his memory of being taken to see *Jurassic Park* as a nine-year-old and being treated to a hamburger afterwards by his mum and dad. As fate would have it, there really was a dinosaur called Byronosaurus.

MAKES 4

INGREDIENTS

1 MEDIUM ONION, VERY FINELY DICED

4 X 180g HAMBURGERS (SEE PAGE 14)

4 BUNS, HALVED

16 GHERKIN SLICES

2½ TBSP BYRON SPICY BBQ SAUCE (SEE PAGE 89)

4 TBSP MAYONNAISE

4 TBSP DRAINED PICKLED JALAPEÑO SLICES (AVAILABLE IN MOST SUPERMARKETS)

8 SLICES OF AMERICAN CHEESE, ROUGHLY THE SAME SIZE AS THE HAMBURGERS

12 SLICES OF CRISPY PANCETTA (SEE PAGE 95)

4 ONION RINGS (SEE PAGE 67)

4 GHERKIN SPEARS

METHOD

1. Bring a medium saucepan of water to the boil and add the diced onion. After 10 seconds, drain through a sieve. Run the sieved onions under the cold tap until cool. Set aside.

2. Preheat the grill to high.

3. Cook the hamburgers to your liking following the instructions on pages 16–17.

4. Meanwhile, toast or grill the cut sides of the buns.

5. Add the blanched onions to the toasted bottom halves of the buns.

6. Top the onions with 4 slices of gherkin and a teaspoon of Byron Spicy BBQ Sauce. Spread another teaspoon of the BBQ Sauce on the top halves of the buns.

7. Spread the mayonnaise on both halves of the buns. Add the jalapeño slices to the top halves of the buns.

8. Once the hamburgers are cooked, transfer to a small roasting tray. Top each one with 2 slices of American cheese and 3 slices of Crispy Pancetta. Place under the hot grill on the highest shelf. Watch carefully and remove the tray from under the grill as soon as the cheese has melted. If using a BBQ, follow the instructions for melting cheese on page 16.

9. Carefully place the hamburgers on the bottom halves of the buns. Top with an Onion Ring and bring the 2 halves together.

10. Serve with a gherkin spear on the side.

MIAMI SLICE

Miami is not just about flash cars, pastel colours and classic 80s TV. This is where we found one of the best and most unusual hamburgers in America – the "frita", which contains crisp shoestring fries. Its undisputed home is El Mago de Las Fritas (The Fritas Wizard), a celebrated burger joint in the city's Little Havana district. It is presided over by a wizened old dude – "El Mago" – who turns out legendary burgers topped with crisp shoestring fries piled inside a Cuban roll, with American cheese and a smokey, spicy sauce. This is our tribute to "The Wizard" and his fritas.

| MAKES 4 |

INGREDIENTS

4 X 180g HAMBURGERS (SEE PAGE 14)

4 BUNS (SOURDOUGH IF POSSIBLE), HALVED

80g SMOKED PAPRIKA KETCHUP (SEE PAGE 82)

100g 'NDUJA (A SPICY ITALIAN SAUSAGE) OR SOBRASADA, THINLY SLICED

8 SLICES OF AMERICAN CHEESE, ROUGHLY THE SAME SIZE AS THE HAMBURGERS

CRISPY POTATOES (SEE PAGE 97)

PORK SCRATCHINGS (SEE PAGE 109)

BYRON HOT SAUCE (SEE PAGE 84)

METHOD

1. Preheat the grill to high.

2. Cook the hamburgers to your liking following the instructions on pages 16–17.

3. Meanwhile, toast or grill the cut sides of the buns.

4. Spread the Smoked Paprika Ketchup over the 8 toasted halves of the buns.

5. When the hamburgers are cooked, transfer to a small roasting tray. Top each one with slices of 'nduja and 2 slices of cheese. Place under the hot grill on the highest shelf. Watch carefully and remove the tray from under the grill as soon as the cheese has melted. If using a BBQ, follow the instructions for melting cheese on page 16.

6. Carefully place the hamburgers on the bottom halves of the buns. Top with the Crispy Potatoes, then bring the 2 halves together.

7. Serve with Pork Scratchings and the Byron Hot Sauce on the side.

ROQUEFORT

Beef and cheese is a classic combination, but beef with blue cheese is a spectacular flavour bomb for the brave. One of our favourites is April Bloomfield's Roquefort burger at The Spotted Pig in New York. In our version, caramelised onions match the strongly flavoured cheese particularly well.

MAKES 4

INGREDIENTS

4 X 180g HAMBURGERS (SEE PAGE 14)

4 BUNS, HALVED

120g MAYONNAISE

¼ ICEBERG LETTUCE, FINELY SHREDDED

120g ROQUEFORT CHEESE, SLICED

CRISPY FRIED ONIONS (SEE PAGE 89)

4 GHERKIN SPEARS

METHOD

1. Preheat the grill to high.

2. Cook the hamburgers to your liking following the instructions on pages 16–17.

3. Meanwhile, toast or grill the cut sides of the buns.

4. Spread the mayonnaise over the top halves of the buns. Add the shredded lettuce to the bottom halves.

5. When the hamburgers are cooked, transfer to a small roasting tray. Top each one with a slice of Roquefort. Place under the hot grill on the highest shelf. Watch carefully and remove the tray from under the grill as soon as the cheese has melted. If using a BBQ, follow the instructions for melting cheese on page 16.

6. Carefully place the hamburgers on the bottom halves of the buns and top with the Crispy Fried Onions.

7. Bring the 2 halves together and serve with a gherkin spear on the side.

CALIFORNIAN

California produces more than 90% of America's avocados, and the fruit features on many of the state's burger menus. Sliced avocado can fall out of a burger, so we strongly recommend using guacamole instead, which adds texture and creaminess and holds together. Pickled red onion is a stalwart of Mexican cuisine that is now very typical in California, too. We use it here instead of a gherkin.

MAKES 4

INGREDIENTS

4 X 180G HAMBURGERS (SEE PAGE 14)

4 BUNS, HALVED

¼ ICEBERG LETTUCE, FINELY SHREDDED

PICKLED RED ONIONS (SEE PAGE 90)

100G BYRON SAUCE (SEE PAGE 88)

⅓ QUANTITY OF GUACAMOLE (SEE PAGE 85)

8 SLICES OF CRISPY SMOKED STREAKY BACON
(SEE PAGE 94)

4 GHERKIN SPEARS

METHOD

1. Preheat the grill to high.

2. Cook the hamburgers to your liking following the instructions on pages 16–17.

3. Meanwhile, toast or grill the cut sides of the buns.

4. Add the shredded lettuce to the bottom halves of the buns.

5. Drain the liquor from the Pickled Red Onions and arrange 5 or 6 onion rings on top of the lettuce.

6. Spoon the Byron Sauce over the onions.

7. When the hamburgers are cooked, place them on top of the sauce.

8. Top the burgers with Guacamole and finish with a 2 slices of Crispy Smoked Streaky Bacon.

9. Bring the 2 halves together and serve with a gherkin spear on the side.

RONALDO

Here's a special we ran during the World Cup in 2014 — a stadium burger as it ought to be.
This is named after a famous Brazilian footballer ("El Fenomeno"), rumoured to be partial to a burger or two.

MAKES 4

INGREDIENTS

8 X 180g HAMBURGERS (SEE PAGE 14)

1 QUANTITY OF BUTTERED ONIONS (SEE PAGE 96)

4 BUNS, HALVED

2 LARGE GHERKINS, SLICED

TOMATO KETCHUP AND AMERICAN MUSTARD

8 SLICES OF AMERICAN CHEESE, ROUGHLY THE SAME SIZE AS THE HAMBURGERS

16 SLICES OF CRISPY PANCETTA (SEE PAGE 95)

100g SHOP-BOUGHT CRISPY ONION PIECES

4 GHERKIN SPEARS

METHOD

1. Preheat the grill to high.

2. Cook the 8 hamburgers to your liking following the instructions on pages 16–17. About 1–2 minutes before they are ready, top with the Buttered Onions.

3. Meanwhile, toast or grill the cut sides of the buns.

4. Place the gherkin slices on the bottom halves of the buns. Squirt a spiral of ketchup and about half as much mustard on both the top and bottom halves of the buns.

5. When the hamburgers are cooked, transfer them to a roasting tray. Top each one with a slice of cheese and 2 slices of Crispy Pancetta. Place under the hot grill on the highest shelf. Watch carefully and remove the tray from under the grill as soon as the cheese has melted.

6. Place 2 hamburgers on the bottom half of each bun and cover completely with the crispy onion pieces.

7. Bring the 2 halves together and serve with a gherkin spear on the side.

UNCLE SAM

This burger emerged effortlessly on a Tuesday morning in June. Our baker had dropped off some glazed buns –
a staple in the US – and we decided to use them in a typical American cheeseburger combo, with American
cheese, sliced pickle, French's mustard and Heinz ketchup. They were so good we put them on the menu in our
Wardour Street restaurant that lunchtime, and sold them all in half an hour. For people of a certain age, the
Uncle Sam patty will rekindle fond memories of their youth; for everyone else, it's just a delicious cheeseburger.

MAKES 4

INGREDIENTS

4 X 180g HAMBURGERS (SEE PAGE 14)

4 BUNS, HALVED

2 LARGE GHERKINS, SLICED

TOMATO KETCHUP AND AMERICAN MUSTARD

8 SLICES OF AMERICAN CHEESE, ROUGHLY THE
SAME SIZE AS THE HAMBURGERS

4 GHERKIN SPEARS

METHOD

1. Preheat the grill to high.

2. Cook the hamburgers to your liking following
the instructions on pages 16–17.

3. Meanwhile, toast or grill the cut sides of
the buns.

4. Place the sliced gherkin on the bottom halves
of the buns. Squirt a spiral of ketchup and
mustard on both halves of the buns.

5. When the hamburgers are cooked, transfer
to a small roasting tray. Top each one with
2 slices of cheese. Place under the hot grill on
the highest shelf. Watch carefully and remove
the tray from under the grill as soon as the
cheese has melted. If using a BBQ, follow the
instructions for melting cheese on page 16.

6. Carefully place the hamburgers on the
bottom halves of the buns.

7. Bring the 2 halves together and serve with
a gherkin spear on the side.

JUICY LUCY

This amazing creation cooks the cheese inside the meat.
Two burger joints in Minneapolis, Minnesota, claim to have invented the Juicy Lucy;
the challenge is to melt the cheese without overcooking the beef.

> MAKES 4

INGREDIENTS

720g CHUCK STEAK, GROUND FOLLOWING THE INSTRUCTIONS ON PAGE 14

8 HOMEMADE CHEESE SLICES (SEE PAGE 94) · 4 BUNS, HALVED

¼ ICEBERG LETTUCE, FINELY SHREDDED · 100g BYRON SAUCE (SEE PAGE 88)

½ BEEF TOMATO, CUT INTO 5mm THICK SLICES · 1 SMALL RED ONION, PEELED AND CUT INTO 2mm THICK RINGS

2 LARGE GHERKINS, SLICED · 4 GHERKIN SPEARS

METHOD

1. Shape the minced steak into 8 x 90g balls. Flatten them following the instructions on page 14, until they are all 12cm wide. They will be thinner than usual.

2. Put a pair of patties on a chopping board and place 2 Homemade Cheese Slices on top of them. Fold over the corners to make the cheese vaguely circular. You should have a hamburger with a small circle of cheese inside, leaving a border of meat about 1cm wide around it.

3. Place the second patty on top. Use your thumb and forefinger to press the edges of the 2 patties, working your way round. Make sure everything is sealed; you don't want any breaks or gaps.

4. Shape the edges of the hamburger, cupping the sides and pressing into your cupped hands, as you would with a normal hamburger. You should be left with a hamburger that is very slightly thicker than usual.

5. Cook the hamburgers following the instructions on pages 16–17, but for a little longer on each side. As you flip the hamburgers, be careful not to tear the meat which will allow the melting cheese centre to escape.

6. Meanwhile, toast or grill the cut sides of the buns.

7. Place the shredded lettuce on the bottom halves of the buns. Spread a spoonful of Byron Sauce on both halves of the buns.

8. Top the lettuce with a slice of tomato. Separate the onion into rings and place 5 of these on top of the tomato.

9. Place the sliced gherkins on the top halves of the buns. When the hamburgers are cooked, carefully place them on the bottom halves of the buns and bring the 2 halves together.

10. Serve with a gherkin spear on the side.

BYRONISSIMO

Here's a light-hearted take on some of the hamburgers we came across in Milan.
The key ingredient is the slow-cooked tomato relish, which has the right level of acidity.
If you find fontina difficult to get hold of, then replace it with Emmenthal.

MAKES 4

INGREDIENTS

4 X 180G HAMBURGERS (SEE PAGE 14)

4 BUNS, HALVED

¼ ICEBERG LETTUCE, FINELY SHREDDED

PICKLED RED ONIONS (SEE PAGE 90)

100G MAYONNAISE

½ BEEF TOMATO, CUT INTO 5MM THICK SLICES

4 TBSP TOMATO RELISH (SEE PAGE 83)

4 SLICES OF FONTINA CHEESE, ABOUT 30G EACH

12 SLICES OF CRISPY PANCETTA (SEE PAGE 95)

4 GHERKIN SPEARS

METHOD

1. Preheat the grill to high.

2. Cook the hamburgers to your liking following the instructions on pages 16–17.

3. Meanwhile, toast or grill the cut sides of the buns.

4. Place the shredded lettuce on the bottom halves of the buns.

5. Drain the liquor from the Pickled Red Onions and place 5 or 6 onion rings on top of the lettuce.

6. Spread a spoonful of mayonnaise on both halves of the buns.

7. When the hamburgers are cooked, transfer to a small roasting tray. Top each one with a slice of tomato and a tablespoonful of the Tomato Relish. Place a slice of cheese on top and press down gently. Top with a slice of Crispy Pancetta.

8. Place under the hot grill on the highest shelf. Watch carefully and remove the tray from under the grill as soon as the cheese has melted. If using a BBQ, follow the instructions for melting cheese on page 16.

9. Place the hamburgers on the bottom halves of the buns and bring the 2 halves together.

10. Serve with a gherkin spear on the side.

RUN RAREBIT RUN

Fred was once charged with making a hamburger that celebrated British ingredients for an event called Meatopia. And what could be more British than Welsh rarebit flavoured with English ale? Think of this as an eccentric English cheeseburger.

MAKES 4

INGREDIENTS

4 X 180G HAMBURGERS (SEE PAGE 14) · 4 BUNS, HALVED · ¼ ICEBERG LETTUCE, FINELY SHREDDED
QUICK PICKLED CUCUMBERS (SEE PAGE 90), OR BREAD & BUTTER PICKLES (SEE PAGE 91)
1 SMALL RED ONION, PEELED AND CUT INTO 2MM THICK RINGS
1 QUANTITY OF WELSH RAREBIT (SEE PAGE 96)
8 SLICES OF CRISPY SMOKED STREAKY BACON (SEE PAGE 94) · 4 GHERKIN SPEARS

FOR THE RAREBIT SAUCE
250G MAYONNAISE · 1½ TBSP ENGLISH MUSTARD · 1½ TBSP WORCESTERSHIRE SAUCE
¼ TSP BYRON HOT SAUCE (SEE PAGE 84), OR YOUR FAVOURITE HOT SAUCE (NOT TABASCO)

METHOD

1. For the rarebit sauce, combine all the ingredients in a small bowl and refrigerate until needed.

2. Preheat the grill to high.

3. Cook the hamburgers to your liking following the instructions on pages 16–17.

4. Meanwhile, toast or grill the cut sides of the buns.

5. Add the shredded lettuce to the bottom halves of the buns and top each with 7 slices of Quick Pickled Cucumber or Bread & Butter Pickles. Separate the onion into rings and place 5 of these on top of the cucumber. Add a spoonful of rarebit sauce to the onions and place another spoonful on the top halves of the buns.

6. When the hamburgers are cooked, transfer to a small roasting tray. Top each hamburger with a slice of Welsh Rarebit. Place under the hot grill on the highest shelf. Watch carefully and remove the tray from under the grill as soon as the cheese has melted. If using a BBQ, follow the instructions for melting cheese on page 16.

7. Carefully place the hamburgers on the bottom halves of the buns and top with 2 slices of the Crispy Smoked Streaky Bacon.

8. Bring the 2 halves together and serve with a gherkin spear on the side.

FLAMING ICEBERG

We love chicken wings glazed in hot sauce, dipped in ranch dressing and served with a crunch of iceberg lettuce (see page 100). One day Fred was thinking: if it works with chicken, then why not with a burger? This is a patty smeared in spicy sauce with plenty of shredded iceberg and cooling ranch dressing.

MAKES 4

INGREDIENTS

4 X 180g HAMBURGERS (SEE PAGE 14) · 4 BUNS, HALVED · ⅓ ICEBERG LETTUCE, FINELY SHREDDED

4 SLICES OF CRISPY SMOKED STREAKY BACON, DICED (SEE PAGE 94) · 6 TBSP RANCH DRESSING (SEE PAGE 82)

120g DRAINED PICKLED JALAPEÑO SLICES, OR TO TASTE

100g SHOP-BOUGHT CRISPY ONION PIECES · 4 GHERKIN SPEARS

FOR THE HOT-SAUCE GLAZE

125g BYRON HOT SAUCE (SEE PAGE 84) · 20ml WHITE WINE VINEGAR

20g UNSALTED BUTTER, CUBED · ¼ TSP CHILLI POWDER

METHOD

1. For the hot-sauce glaze, put a small saucepan over a medium–high heat and add the Byron Hot Sauce and vinegar. Bring to the boil. Add the butter and chilli powder and whisk until the butter has melted.

2. Blitz the glaze in a food processor or using a stick blender until completely smooth. Leave to cool.

3. Cook the hamburgers to your liking following the instructions on pages 16–17.

4. Meanwhile, toast or grill the cut sides of the buns.

5. Place the shredded lettuce on the bottom halves of the buns. Sprinkle the diced Crispy Smoked Streaky Bacon on top. Spoon 1 tablespoon of the Ranch Dressing over the lettuce and bacon, and spread a little more Ranch Dressing over the top halves of the buns.

6. Add the jalapeño slices to the top halves of the buns.

7. Spoon a little glaze on the bottom halves of the buns. Put the rest of the glaze in a large bowl.

8. When the hamburgers are cooked, transfer them to the bowl of glaze. Turn them in the glaze until completely coated.

9. Carefully place the glazed hamburgers on the bottom halves of the buns and cover completely with the crispy onion pieces.

10. Bring the 2 halves together and serve with a gherkin spear on the side.

FREDDAR DAWG

"Freddar" is Fred's take on American cheese, and this recipe showcases it like nothing else in the book. It was inspired by the burger at Father's Office in Santa Monica, Los Angeles, which is served in a baguette with rocket. We were suspicious at first, but we had to grudgingly admit that it was the best burger we had enjoyed in the city.

MAKES 4

INGREDIENTS

1 MEDIUM ONION, PEELED AND VERY FINELY DICED

4 X 180G HAMBURGERS (SEE PAGE 14)

4 HOT DOG BUNS, HALVED LENGTHWAYS

⅓ ICEBERG LETTUCE, FINELY SHREDDED

4 TSP BYRON SAUCE (SEE PAGE 88)

1 LARGE GHERKIN, SLICED

AMERICAN MUSTARD

4 HOMEMADE CHEESE SLICES (SEE PAGE 94)

16 SLICES OF CRISPY PANCETTA, FINELY CHOPPED (SEE PAGE 95)

4 GHERKIN SPEARS

METHOD

1. Bring a medium saucepan of water to the boil and add the diced onion. Simmer for 10 seconds, then drain through a sieve. Run the onions under a cold tap until cool, then set aside.

2. Preheat the grill to high.

3. Cook the hamburgers to your liking following the instructions on pages 16–17.

4. Meanwhile, toast or grill the cut sides of the hot dog buns.

5. Place the shredded lettuce on the bottom halves of the buns and top with a spoonful of the onions and a teaspoon of Byron Sauce.

6. Drizzle American mustard over the top halves of the buns and add the sliced gherkin.

7. When the hamburgers are cooked, transfer to a small roasting tray. Top each one with a Homemade Cheese Slice. Place under the hot grill on the highest shelf. Watch carefully and remove the tray from under the grill as soon as the cheese has melted. If using a BBQ, follow the instructions for melting cheese on page 16.

8. Cut the cheese-topped hamburgers in half and place on the bottom halves of the hot dog buns.

9. Sprinkle the Crispy Pancetta over the hamburgers and fold the burger dogs together.

10. Serve with a gherkin spear on the side.

PATTY MELT

This is a classic US diner dish – the mutant offspring of a cheese toastie and a hamburger. It seems to have originated in the 1940s or 1950s at a chain of Californian coffee shops called Tiny Naylors, run by William "Tiny" Naylor (he was anything but, apparently). Fred's Patty Melt consists of two slices of buttered rye bread which sandwich a coarsely minced beef patty, sweet red onions and Swiss cheese. Sliced brioche, widely available in supermarkets, and Homemade Cheese Slices make great substitutes.

> MAKES 4

INGREDIENTS

450g CHUCK STEAK, GROUND FOLLOWING THE INSTRUCTIONS ON PAGE 14

8 SLICES OF BRIOCHE BREAD

8 HOMEMADE CHEESE SLICES (SEE PAGE 94), OR 8 SLICES OF AMERICAN CHEESE

SOFT UNSALTED BUTTER, FOR SPREADING

OLIVE OIL

FOR THE ONIONS

25g UNSALTED BUTTER

2 MEDIUM RED ONIONS, VERY FINELY DICED

FINE SEA SALT

METHOD

1. For the onions, heat a small saucepan over a medium–low heat. Add the butter, then the finely diced onion and a pinch of salt. Cover with a lid and cook for 30 minutes, stirring occasionally, until the onions are very soft.

2. Meanwhile, separate the ground chuck into 4 balls.

3. When the onions are cooked, place a large frying pan over a medium heat, add a dash of oil and add the meatballs to the hot pan, flattening each one with a fish slice or spatula until 1.5cm thick. Raise the heat to medium–high and fry for 2 minutes on each side or until cooked to your liking.

4. Spread a heaped teaspoon of the softened onions out onto each slice of bread. Top with the Homemade Cheese Slices.

5. Sandwich the 4 patties between the bread.

6. Spread a layer of butter over the top sides of each sandwich.

7. Wipe clean the pan that you cooked the patties in, and heat over a medium–low flame.

8. Add the sandwiches to the pan, butter side down. Spread a layer of butter over the now-top side of the sandwiches. Cook for 1 minute, pressing down gently with a fish slice or spatula, then turn and cook on the other side for a further minute. By this point, both sides should now be golden and the cheese runny.

9. Slice in half and serve immediately. Byron Sauce is an ideal accompaniment.

CHICKEN

Substituting chicken for beef can make for a delicious and lighter alternative to a regular burger.
We're not fans of minced chicken, however, which lacks the texture and succulence of a whole breast.
Marinating chicken in seasoned buttermilk (see page 143) keeps it juicy, essential for grilling over fierce heat.

MAKES 4

INGREDIENTS

4 BUNS, HALVED

100G BYRON SAUCE (SEE PAGE 88)

4 LETTUCE LEAVES, SUCH AS ESCAROLE, LOLLO VERDE
OR CURLY LEAF GREEN LETTUCE

½ BEEF TOMATO, CUT INTO 5MM THICK SLICES

1 SMALL RED ONION, PEELED AND SLICED INTO
2MM THICK RINGS

4 CHAR-GRILLED MARINATED CHICKEN BREASTS
(SEE PAGE 143)

4 GHERKIN SPEARS

METHOD

1. Toast or grill the cut sides of the buns.

2. Spread the Byron Sauce evenly over the top
halves of the buns.

3. Place one leaf of lettuce on top of the sauce,
then add a slice of tomato. Separate the onion
into rings and place 5 on top of each.

4. Once the Char-grilled Marinated Chicken
Breasts are cooked, carefully place them on the
bottom halves of the buns.

5. Bring the 2 halves together and serve with a
gherkin spear on the side.

VEGGIE MUSHROOM & GOAT'S CHEESE

The mere mention of "vegetarian" can send some burger lovers apoplectic. But vegetarian customers are as passionate about their burgers as meat lovers are. Opinion seems to be divided between devotees of the "patty" experience and those who prefer a combination of vegetables. Here's one which satisfies the latter, with a heartier patty on page 56.

MAKES 4

INGREDIENTS

4 LARGE PORTOBELLO MUSHROOMS

2 ROASTED RED PEPPERS AT ROOM TEMPERATURE – SHOP-BOUGHT AND DRAINED, OR SEE RECIPE ON PAGE 95

4 X 1cm THICK SLICES OF RIND-ON GOAT'S CHEESE, E.G. A WIDE, SOFT-RIPENED CHÈVRE BLANC

4 BUNS, HALVED

100g AÏOLI (SEE PAGE 84)

50g BABY SPINACH LEAVES

½ BEEF TOMATO, CUT INTO 5mm THICK SLICES

1 SMALL RED ONION, PEELED AND SLICED INTO 2mm THICK RINGS

OLIVE OIL

SEA SALT AND FRESHLY GROUND BLACK PEPPER

4 GHERKIN SPEARS

METHOD

1. Preheat the oven to 180°C (350°F).

2. Snap off the stalks of the mushrooms and discard. Place the mushroom caps onto a baking tray. Drizzle with a little olive oil and season with salt and pepper.

3. Roast the mushrooms for 15 minutes or until softened. These will keep in the fridge for up to 2 days.

4. When you are ready to cook the burgers, cut the peppers in half and place a piece on top of each mushroom. Top with the goat's cheese.

5. Preheat a grill or BBQ to high. If using a grill, place the topped mushrooms, still on their baking tray, under the grill on the highest shelf. Watch carefully and remove the tray from under the grill as soon as the cheese has melted. If using a BBQ, place the mushrooms on a grate, close the lid and cook until the cheese has melted.

6. Meanwhile, toast or grill the cut sides of the buns.

7. Spread the Aïoli over the top halves of the buns.

8. Place the spinach leaves on the aïoli, then top with a slice of tomato. Separate the onion into rings and place 5 of these on top of each tomato.

9. Carefully place the topped mushrooms on the bottom halves of the buns.

10. Bring the 2 halves together and serve with a gherkin spear on the side.

VEGGIE BEAN

This pulsed "patty" is made special with the crunch of panko breadcrumbs.

MAKES 4

INGREDIENTS

4 BUNS, HALVED · 80g BYRON SAUCE (SEE PAGE 88) · 80g AÏOLI (SEE PAGE 84)

50g BABY SPINACH LEAVES · ½ BEEF TOMATO, CUT INTO 5mm THICK SLICES

1 SMALL RED ONION, PEELED AND SLICED INTO 2mm THICK RINGS · 4 GHERKIN SPEARS

2 ROASTED RED PEPPERS AT ROOM TEMPERATURE – SHOP-BOUGHT AND DRAINED, OR SEE RECIPE ON PAGE 95

FOR THE PATTIES

200g DRAINED CANNED CHICKPEAS, RINSED · 200g DRAINED CANNED KIDNEY BEANS, RINSED

1 BUNCH OF FRESH CORIANDER, LEAVES ROUGHLY CHOPPED · 2 TSP GROUND CUMIN

2 TSP SWEET SMOKED PAPRIKA · 2½ TSP CASTER SUGAR · 1 TSP FINE SEA SALT

120g PLAIN FLOUR · 140g DRAINED CANNED SWEETCORN, WASHED

2 MEDIUM EGGS, BEATEN · 120g PANKO OR DRIED WHITE BREADCRUMBS

SUNFLOWER OR VEGETABLE OIL, FOR SHALLOW FRYING

METHOD

1. For the patties, place three-quarters of the chickpeas, three-quarters of the kidney beans, all the coriander, the cumin, paprika, sugar, salt and one-third of the flour into a food processor and blend until you have a coarse paste.

2. Place the remaining chickpeas and kidney beans in a bowl and roughly mash with a fork or potato masher. Spoon the paste from the food processor into the mixing bowl, along with the sweetcorn, and mix well.

3. Divide the mixture into 4 equal portions and shape into patties as you would for hamburgers (see page 14). Refrigerate for an hour or so.

4. Place the remaining flour, eggs and breadcrumbs in 3 shallow bowls.

5. Dip each patty in the flour until evenly coated and then shake off any excess. Next, dip each patty into the beaten eggs, coating well and allowing any excess to drip off. Finally, turn each patty in the breadcrumbs until completely covered. Transfer the prepared

patties to a plate. When ready to cook, heat a large, deep frying pan over a medium–high heat. Heat 1cm of oil in it.

6. Meanwhile, toast or grill the cut sides of the buns. When the oil is hot, fry the patties for 2 minutes on each side.

7. Add the Byron Sauce to the bottom halves of the buns. Spread the Aïoli over the top halves.

8. Place the spinach leaves over the aïoli, then top with a slice of tomato. Separate the onion into rings and place 5 of these on top of each tomato.

9. Carefully place the bean burgers on the bottom half of each bun. Cut the peppers in half and place a piece on top of each burger.

10. Bring the 2 halves together and serve with a gherkin spear on the side.

BURGER BUNS

These are excellent burger buns: soft and squidgy, with just the right amount of "give".
They're well worth the time and effort they take: you'll notice the difference from the first bite.

INGREDIENTS

3 TBSP WARM MILK, PLUS A DASH FOR THE EGG WASH · 200ML WARM WATER · 1 TSP DRY ACTIVE YEAST
25G CASTER SUGAR · 400G STRONG WHITE BREAD FLOUR
50G PLAIN FLOUR, PLUS EXTRA FOR DUSTING
1 TBSP VITAMIN C POWDER (OPTIONAL, FOR A LIGHTER, FLUFFIER BUN) · 1½ TSP FINE SEA SALT
35G COLD UNSALTED BUTTER, FINELY CUBED · 2 MEDIUM EGGS

METHOD

1. In a small mixing bowl, mix the warm milk, water, yeast and sugar. Set aside for 5 minutes or until frothy.

2. Meanwhile, put the flours, vitamin C powder, if using, salt and butter in a large mixing bowl. Rub the butter into the flour until the mixture resembles breadcrumbs.

3. Lightly beat one of the eggs and add to the flour along with the yeast mixture. Stir until a wet dough forms.

4. Tip the dough out onto a floured work surface and knead until elastic and smooth, about 15 minutes. It will be quite wet at the beginning but keep going.

5. Shape the dough into a ball and return to the mixing bowl. Cover with a piece of oiled clingfilm and leave in a warm place until doubled in size. This can take 2–3 hours depending on the temperature of your kitchen. Alternatively, prove overnight in the fridge.

6. Tip the dough out onto a floured work surface and "punch down" to deflate it. Separate it into 8 pieces. To make sure all your buns are exactly the same size, you can weigh the whole quantity of dough first, and then each of the 8 portions should be an eighth of the original weight.

7. Roll each piece of dough very gently into a ball, tucking in any edges. The tops of the balls should be smooth, with any sealed edges on the underside.

8. Space the balls about 3cm apart on 2 baking trays lined with non-stick parchment paper and cover loosely with clingfilm, making sure they are free to rise.

9. Leave to rise in a warm place for at least 3 hours, or up to 7. The longer you leave them to prove, the fluffier and lighter they will be, but if left for too long they will collapse. They should be 4 times their original size. Shortly before the buns are ready to bake, preheat the oven to 200°C (400°F).

10. Beat the remaining egg with a dash of milk to make a glaze. Gently brush the tops of the buns with the glaze. Place a shallow roasting tray or baking dish filled with a 3cm depth of water in the bottom of the hot oven to create steam.

11. Bake the buns in the preheated oven for 12–15 minutes, turning the trays round halfway through, if necessary, to ensure even cooking.

12. When cooked, remove the buns from the oven and leave to cool completely on the trays. Eat once cool, or store in an airtight container for up to 2 days.

CHAPTER 2

Fries & Sides

I can't imagine eating a burger without fries: they are the ultimate finger food. If a bun is mainly a vehicle to deliver the patty, then these thin strands of potato are the genuine carbohydrates to accompany the protein. Britain may be a nation of chip-lovers: we tend to favour the thicker, fluffier innards of a fried potato over its crisp exterior. But, perhaps unpatriotically, I have to admit that French fries are the proper companion for a hamburger and, in the restaurants, we sell twice as many of them as we do our "skin-on chips".

However, burgers go with other things too. The huge popularity of our courgette fries was a welcome surprise to me: I first offered them partly because they reminded me of my days running Italian restaurants. I wasn't sure if they would fly, but now I think our customers would rise in revolt if we tried to remove them. They're a little lighter than fries, and they're also somewhat quicker and easier to make.

Many of these sides stand alone, of course:
macaroni cheese is a fine Sunday-night dinner in its own right;
the baked sweet potato chips with green chilli are a great
movie-night snack; and the coleslaw and onion rings,
I like to think, are masterclasses in how to do those dishes.

We realise that many people don't feel they have time to make their own French fries. If you do go down the ready-made route, buy frozen fries that have very few ingredients: just potato, some fat and a little salt. If possible, fry them in a deep saucepan or a proper fryer. If you must bake them, toss them in a little beef dripping before putting them in the oven. The best non-chip "chips" here come from sweet potato. They're baked, healthier and easy – and your guests will appreciate the effort.

French Fries

This is quicker and easier than other recipes, but still makes a cracking fry.

INGREDIENTS

1.7kg LARGE MARIS PIPER POTATOES

VEGETABLE OIL, FOR DEEP FRYING

FINE SEA SALT

METHOD

1. Peel the potatoes and slice them into French fries 0.75cm thick.

2. Rinse the fries for up to 10 minutes under cold water, or until the water runs clear. Drain well.

3. Heat a deep-fat fryer to 150°C (300°F), or pour enough oil into a large, deep saucepan to come one-third of the way up the sides. Heat the oil over a medium heat until it reaches 150°C (300°F). A cooking thermometer is useful but not essential. (A cube of white bread will brown in 70 seconds if the oil is at the right temperature.)

4. Cook the fries, in batches, in the hot oil for 5 minutes, or until very lightly coloured and soft. Carefully remove the fries using a slotted spoon or "spider" (setting aside the oil for later) and drain in a single layer on kitchen paper. Chill them in the fridge.

5. Reheat the oil to 180°C (350°F). (A cube of white bread will brown in 40 seconds if the oil is at the right temperature.) Cook the fries, in batches, in the hot oil for 2½–3 minutes or until gold and crunchy.

6. Carefully remove the fries and drain in a single layer on kitchen paper. Serve immediately, sprinkled with a little salt.

Chips

A proudly British chip which we'd never take off the menu.

INGREDIENTS

1.7kg LARGE MARIS PIPER POTATOES, SCRUBBED CLEAN

VEGETABLE OIL, FOR DEEP FRYING

SEA SALT

METHOD

1. Slice the unpeeled potatoes into chips 1.75cm thick.

2. Rinse the chips for up to 10 minutes under cold water, or until the water runs clear. Drain well.

3. Place the chips in a large saucepan of cold, salted water. Bring to the boil and simmer for 8–10 minutes until the chips are tender but not breaking up. Drain and leave to cool.

4. Heat a deep-fat fryer to 150°C (300°F), or pour enough oil into a large, deep saucepan to come one-third of the way up the sides. Heat the oil over a medium heat until it reaches 150°C (300°F). A cooking thermometer is useful but not essential. (A cube of white bread will brown in 70 seconds if the oil is at the right temperature.)

5. Cook the chips, in batches, in the hot oil for 3 minutes, or until very lightly coloured. Carefully remove the chips using a slotted spoon or "spider" (setting aside the oil for later) and drain in a single layer on kitchen paper. Refrigerate until cool.

6. Reheat the oil to 180°C (350°F). (A cube of white bread will brown in 40 seconds if the oil is at the right temperature.) Cook the chips, in batches, in the hot oil for 2½–3 minutes or until gold and crunchy.

7. Carefully remove the chips and drain in a single layer on kitchen paper. Serve immediately, sprinkled with a little salt.

Seasoned Fries

SERVES 4

*Seasoned fries always remind us of the Deep South. There's a chicken chain there called Bojangles,
where they serve fries with a shaker that contains peppers, salt and a little sugar.*

METHOD

1 QUANTITY OF HOT FRENCH FRIES
(SEE PAGE 64)

For the seasoning

1 TSP GROUND BLACK PEPPER

1 TSP GROUND WHITE PEPPER

1 TSP HOT SMOKED PAPRIKA

1 TSP SWEET SMOKED PAPRIKA

1 TSP ONION POWDER

¼ TSP GARLIC POWDER

2 TSP FINE SEA SALT

INGREDIENTS

1. Mix all the seasoning ingredients together.

2. In a large mixing bowl, toss the hot French Fries in half the seasoning. Taste and add a little more seasoning, if needed. Any leftover seasoning can be stored in a clean airtight container.

3. Serve the fries immediately.

WHEN LIFE GIVES YOU LEMONS...

TALL TALE
№ 01

I've got an old friend who knows a lot more about the world of property than I do. He's always been a trusted and generous advisor, but I take particular pleasure in remembering the one time he was wrong. And thank goodness he was.

Location is everything in the restaurant business, and we had just signed up for the site that would become the very first Byron, at 222 Kensington High Street in west London. I was a bundle of excitement (and nerves) – but he was less thrilled. "I'm telling you, Tom. That site will never work," he cautioned.

"It's a lemon – the signs are all there. I suggest you back out of the deal."

We couldn't. It was full steam ahead, and all we could do was throw everything (including several kitchen sinks) at making that restaurant work. The rest is hamburger history – and every Christmas, I'm always sure to send my friend a card reminding him how welcome he is to stop by for a bite to eat (...or perhaps a nice cold Byron lager) at no. 222 Kensington High Street, eight years and millions of hamburgers later.

Onion Rings

SERVES 4

A good onion ring is surprisingly tricky to get right.
You need a batter that seizes in the oil so that the onion steams and sweetens inside.
These are lots of fun to eat.

INGREDIENTS

1 LARGE WHITE ONION

VEGETABLE OIL, FOR DEEP FRYING

For the beer batter

180g PLAIN FLOUR

2 TSP CAJUN SPICE/SEASONING

330ml BEER

FINE SEA SALT AND FRESHLY GROUND
BLACK PEPPER

For dusting

100g PLAIN FLOUR

2 TBSP POLENTA OR CORNMEAL

METHOD

1. Trim the onion, then slice into 1.5cm thick rings. Remove the skin and discard the first layer. Separate the slices into rings.

2. For the beer batter, put the flour and Cajun spice/seasoning in a large mixing bowl with ¼ teaspoon salt and 4–5 grinds of pepper. Pour in the beer and whisk with a fork or balloon whisk until combined.

3. Heat a deep-fat fryer to 180°C (350°F), or pour enough oil into a large, deep saucepan to come one-third of the way up the sides. Heat the oil over a medium heat until it reaches 180°C (350°F). A cooking thermometer is useful but not essential. (A cube of white bread will brown in 40 seconds if the oil is at the right temperature.)

4. While the oil is heating, mix the ingredients for the dusting in a large bowl. Season with 1 teaspoon salt and a couple of grinds of pepper.

5. When the oil is at the right temperature, dip the onion rings into the dusting, shake off any excess and then dip into the batter until evenly coated.

6. Cook the onion rings, in batches, in the hot oil for 2–3 minutes until golden underneath, then carefully turn the rings over with a slotted spoon or "spider", and cook for a further 2–3 minutes or until dark golden all over.

7. Carefully remove the onion rings with the slotted spoon or "spider" and drain in a single layer on kitchen paper. Keep warm while you repeat the process with the remaining rings. Serve as soon as possible.

Macaroni Cheese

SERVES 4-6

*We have strong views about this dish. Done well it is a revelation, but poor versions are unfailingly disappointing.
The pasta must be al dente, the sauce sufficiently cheesy, and the topping must have good colour
and a definite chewiness. Fred dedicates this recipe to his grandmother, who was a fine cook.
Of all her dishes, this is the one he keeps coming back to.*

INGREDIENTS

400ɢ MACARONI

100ɢ GRATED MATURE CHEDDAR CHEESE

SEA SALT

For the cheese sauce

400ᴍʟ WHOLE MILK

2 TBSP CORNFLOUR

100ᴍʟ DOUBLE CREAM

75ɢ GRATED MATURE CHEDDAR CHEESE

50ɢ GRATED PARMESAN CHEESE

METHOD

1. Preheat the grill to medium–high.

2. Cook the macaroni in a large pan of salted, boiling water for 10 minutes, or according to the packet instructions. Drain and set aside.

3. For the cheese sauce, mix together 2 tablespoons of the milk with the cornflour in a small bowl until smooth. Put the rest of the milk, and the cream, in a medium saucepan over a medium heat and simmer for a minute, making sure it doesn't boil.

4. After 3–4 minutes, pour the cornflour mixture into the milk, whisking continuously. Stir in the Cheddar and Parmesan and continue to whisk for 3–4 minutes until the cheese has melted and the sauce is smooth and slightly thickened.

5. Mix the cheese sauce and macaroni, stirring gently to ensure the pasta is coated. Transfer to an ovenproof dish.

6. Scatter the remaining 100g grated Cheddar over the macaroni cheese. Place under the preheated grill for about 5 minutes, or until the top is melted, bubbling and golden. Keep an eye on it, as cheese can burn quickly. Remove from the grill and serve.

Macaroni Cheese Hash Browns

SERVES 4–6

Serve these when you have friends round.
They will make everyone smile.

INGREDIENTS

300g MACARONI

VEGETABLE OIL, FOR DEEP FRYING

100g PLAIN FLOUR

2 MEDIUM EGGS, LIGHTLY BEATEN

200g PANKO OR DRIED WHITE BREADCRUMBS

A DASH OF WHOLE MILK

SEA SALT

For the cheese sauce

400ml DOUBLE CREAM

24 SLICES OF AMERICAN CHEESE
(480g IN TOTAL)

150g GRATED CHEDDAR CHEESE

180g FINELY GRATED PARMESAN CHEESE

METHOD

1. Cook the macaroni in salted, boiling water for 1 minute less than recommended on the packet instructions.

2. For the cheese sauce, heat the cream in a medium–large saucepan until steaming. Add the American cheese, Cheddar and Parmesan and whisk with a fork or balloon whisk over a low heat until the cheese has melted and the sauce is smooth. Do not let the mixture bubble.

3. Drain the macaroni, then stir into the warm cheese sauce and cook gently over a medium–low heat for a further minute. Remove from the heat.

4. Line a lipped baking tray with non-stick parchment paper, and pour the macaroni cheese onto it. Spread it to the edges and top with another layer of parchment paper. Refrigerate until cooled and set (about 2 hours).

5. When you are ready to start cooking, heat a deep-fat fryer to 180°C (350°F), or pour enough oil into a large, deep saucepan to come one-third of the way up the sides. Heat the oil over a medium heat until it reaches 180°C (350°F). A cooking thermometer is useful but not essential. (A cube of white bread will brown in 40 seconds if the oil is at the right temperature.)

6. Remove the macaroni cheese from the fridge and cut into triangles about 7cm tall on the longest side, and 4cm long on the 2 shorter sides.

7. Put the flour, eggs and breadcrumbs in 3 separate, wide, shallow bowls. Add a dash of milk to the beaten eggs and mix.

8. Dip each macaroni triangle into the flour until evenly coated, and then shake off any excess. Next, dip each triangle into the egg, allowing any excess egg to drip off. Finally, turn each triangle in the breadcrumbs until completely coated. Transfer the macaroni triangles to a large plate or tray.

9. Cook the triangles, in batches, in the hot oil for 2–2½ minutes until golden on the outside and gooey in the middle (be careful checking for gooeyness – the melted cheese will be hot!).

10. Carefully remove the macaroni triangles with a slotted spoon or "spider" and drain in a single layer on kitchen paper. Serve immediately.

Chile Chilli Cheese Fries

SERVES 4

Take a deep breath before you start eating this:
slow-cooked beef shin, chopped and mixed with roast peppers and seasoning,
with plenty of chillies for spice and heat, slathered on French fries and topped with cheese.

INGREDIENTS

1 QUANTITY OF HOT FRENCH FRIES (SEE PAGE 64)

¼ QUANTITY OF BEEF CHILLI (SEE PAGE 118), HEATED THROUGH

4 HOMEMADE CHEESE SLICES (SEE PAGE 94), BROKEN UP A LITTLE

4 LONG GREEN CHILLIES, VERY THINLY SLICED

CHIPOTLE MAYO (SEE PAGE 88)

1 SMALL BUNCH OF CORIANDER, LEAVES ONLY

For the lime-marinated onions

1 MEDIUM RED ONION, PEELED AND FINELY DICED

JUICE OF 3 LIMES

PINCH OF FINE SEA SALT

METHOD

1. For the lime-marinated onions, mix the ingredients in a non-reactive bowl. Cover and marinate for at least 30 minutes, or up to 3 days.

2. When you are ready to start cooking, preheat the grill to high.

3. Place half the hot French Fries in a baking dish (approx. 25 x 20cm). Top with half the Beef Chilli, dotting it over the fries. Dot half the broken Homemade Cheese Slices over the top. Sprinkle over half the sliced chillies.

4. Top all this with the remaining fries and repeat the beef chilli, cheese and chilli layers. Grill for 1½–2 minutes or until the cheese has melted.

5. Remove from the grill and spoon the Chipotle Mayo over the dish. Drain the marinated onions and sprinkle over the top, along with the coriander. Serve immediately.

CLOCKING IN

TALL TALE
Nº 02

Whichever Byron you're in — from the distressed, deliberately unfinished feel of Islington to the pastel shades of Putney — you'll notice a clock dominating the décor. All our restaurants are individually designed; the clock is one of the few things that they have in common — a Byron motif, if you will.

I've always had a bit of a thing for clocks — they're the perfect blend of form and function. Stylish, simple, effective. But really, when we were a few days off opening our first restaurant, we just needed a way to tell the time. So I drove to Andrew Nebbett in St. John's Wood, purveyor of fine antiques

to well-heeled Londoners, maxed out my credit card on a handsome old station clock, and then realised I had no idea how to get it home.

I just about managed to fit the thing in the back of my car. It survived its rather undignified journey intact and has hung on the wall in Kensington, looking down on us all, to this day. Now every time we open a restaurant and come up with a brand new design, we launch into another hunt for a beautiful old clock as a finishing touch (although Kensington's will always be my favourite). These days, luckily, I don't have to worry about fitting it in the car.

Courgette Fries

SERVES 4

These are a simple and easy twist on the zucchine fritte *beloved of Italian restaurants.*
They are wildly popular in our restaurants and there would be outrage if we ever removed them.
We enjoy them dipped in BBQ sauce or Ranch Dressing (see page 82).

INGREDIENTS

3 COURGETTES, ENDS TRIMMED

VEGETABLE OIL, FOR DEEP FRYING

For the flour mix

400g PLAIN FLOUR

100g POLENTA OR CORNMEAL

FINE SEA SALT AND FRESHLY GROUND
BLACK PEPPER

For the batter

300ml BUTTERMILK

1 TSP CASTER SUGAR

1 TSP BYRON HOT SAUCE (SEE PAGE 84),
OR YOUR FAVOURITE HOT SAUCE

METHOD

1. Cut each courgette in half to create 2 shorter cylinders. Cut these in half lengthways. Now cut all 4 pieces into roughly 5mm thick sticks that resemble fries.

2. For the flour mix, combine the flour and polenta or cornmeal in a large bowl and season with 2 teaspoons salt and a couple of grinds of pepper.

3. For the batter, mix the ingredients together.

4. Heat a deep-fat fryer to 180°C (350°F), or pour enough oil into a large, deep saucepan to come one-third of the way up the sides. Heat the oil over a medium heat until it reaches 180°C (350°F). A cooking thermometer is useful but not essential. (A cube of white bread will brown in 40 seconds if the oil is at the right temperature.)

5. When the oil is ready, dip the courgette pieces in the batter, then in the flour mix and make sure that each is well coated.

6. Cook the courgette pieces, in batches, in the hot oil for 3–3½ minutes until golden and crisp.

7. Carefully remove the fries with a slotted spoon or "spider" and drain in a single layer on kitchen paper.

8. Just before serving, season the fries with a little salt, tossing to coat evenly. Serve immediately.

Baked Sweet Potato Chips with Green Chilli

SERVES 4

This is one of the best and simplest recipes in this book.
We love the combination of nutty sweet potato with the fragrant heat of green chilli.

INGREDIENTS

3 MEDIUM, SWEET POTATOES (APPROX. 800-900g IN TOTAL), SCRUBBED CLEAN

2 TBSP OLIVE OIL

1 TSP FINE SEA SALT

2 LONG GREEN CHILLIES, VERY THINLY SLICED

METHOD

1. Preheat the oven to 190°C (375°F).

2. Slice the unpeeled potatoes into chips 1cm thick.

3. Put the chips in a large mixing bowl, toss with the olive oil and season with salt.

4. Spread the chips out in a single layer on a large, non-stick baking tray – or use 2 baking trays if necessary. Bake in the preheated oven for 20 minutes, then turn the chips over and bake for a further 20 minutes, or until browned and crisp around the edges.

5. Remove the chips from the oven, place in a serving bowl and add the sliced chillies. Toss briefly and serve.

Whipped Potatoes

SERVES 4

*Most people expect the potatoes that come with their burger to be chipped and fried, not mashed.
But in the diners and cafés of the Deep South, a particularly buttery version of mash,
known as whipped potatoes, is a popular accompaniment to a hamburger.
This is our take on it – and remember, don't hold back on the butter.*

INGREDIENTS

1kg DESIREE OR OTHER WAXY POTATO, PEELED

250g UNSALTED BUTTER, CUBED

75ml WHOLE MILK

75ml DOUBLE CREAM

SEA SALT AND FRESHLY GROUND BLACK PEPPER

METHOD

1. Cut the peeled potatoes in half or quarters so that they are all evenly sized. Rinse under cold running water for about 5 minutes, or until the water runs clear. Drain.

2. Place the potatoes in a large saucepan of cold water. Season the water with lots of salt – about 3 tablespoons. Bring to the boil, then reduce the heat and simmer gently until the potatoes are absolutely tender – this will probably take about 25 minutes, but check.

3. Drain the potatoes in a colander and leave them to steam-dry for 3–4 minutes. Rinse and dry the saucepan.

4. Place a fine sieve over the clean saucepan and push the potatoes, one by one, through the sieve using a spatula or wooden spoon. You're aiming to create small rice-sized pieces of potato. This method means you're guaranteed no lumps.

5. When all the potatoes have been "sieved", place the pan back on a low heat. Add the butter and stir while it melts. Beat the melted butter into the potato with the spatula or wooden spoon.

6. When everything is incorporated, beat in the milk and cream. Taste and adjust the seasoning. You probably won't need much salt. Serve immediately.

BYRON ON TOUR

Some months after we first started out – and we had all been working non-stop for about as long as we could remember – we decided we needed a break. A hamburger-heavy break, maybe, but a break nonetheless. So everyone involved in running the show – ten of us back then – took off to NYC for four days of carefree eating, drinking and exploring.

Fast forward a few years to the present day and our numbers have swelled somewhat, but we still like to get away for a bit of R&R. These days, more than 100 of us come along on what has come to be known as our annual "Big Trip", and we don't plan on breaking the habit any time soon.

But no matter how many of us get on that plane, there will only ever be two rules: stay out of casualty, and stay out of custody.

So far? So good. Just.

Coleslaw

SERVES 4

No apple, fennel or curry powder here.
This is well-seasoned, accessible and refreshing coleslaw - just as it should be.

INGREDIENTS

300g MAYONNAISE

1 TBSP WHITE WINE VINEGAR

½ TSP CASTER SUGAR

½ TSP SEA SALT

½ WHITE CABBAGE, CORE REMOVED AND LEAVES FINELY SHREDDED

3 CARROTS, PEELED AND GRATED

FRESHLY GROUND BLACK PEPPER

METHOD

1. In a large mixing bowl, mix the mayonnaise, vinegar, sugar, salt and a couple of grinds of pepper until combined.

2. Add the cabbage and grated carrot and mix, making sure every bit of vegetable is coated. You may prefer to do this by hand. Taste and adjust the seasoning.

3. Serve immediately or refrigerate in an airtight container for up to 2 days. Stir before serving.

CHAPTER 3

SAUCES, TOPPINGS, DIPS & PICKLES

No matter how succulent the meat, a burger needs sauce: a lick of flavour to balance the other components. This is where you add accents and can personalise with classic burger sauce, the dark smokiness of barbecue, the piquant heat of chipotle mayo or the funk of blue cheese.

Mayonnaise is sometimes enough: it provides a whisper of flavour and much in the way of texture. But I find myself invariably coming back to our Byron Sauce (see page 88), which has the reassuring, sweet-sour familiarity of ketchup, the smoothness of mayo and some complementary crunch from chopped pickle.

SOME PEOPLE PREFER TO LIFT THE TOP HALF OF THE BUN AND SHAKE OVER THE SAUCE THEMSELVES. OTHERS, INCLUDING ME, ARE PROUD BURGER-DUNKERS.

In this chapter, we've also included several things you can add to a burger that will work to enhance it: the sugar-vinegar crunch of homemade pickles, a dollop of guacamole (much better than sliced avocado, which can fall out of a burger), and a fresh tomato relish. We serve a wedge of pickled cucumber on the side at Byron: it's a diner classic as well as a refreshing palate cleanser between bites. Don't forget that many of these dips work equally well for fries, onion rings and other sides.

Ranch Dressing

SERVES 4

An ever-popular American dressing.

INGREDIENTS

250g MAYONNAISE

120ml BUTTERMILK

½ TSP ONION POWDER

¼ TSP GARLIC POWDER

JUICE OF ¾ LEMON

SEA SALT AND FRESHLY GROUND BLACK PEPPER

METHOD

1. Mix all the ingredients and add a couple of pinches of salt and a twist of pepper. Taste and adjust the seasoning as necessary.

2. Use immediately or refrigerate in an airtight container for up to 4 days.

Smoked Paprika Ketchup

SERVES 4

Here's a secret: pimping shop-bought ketchup is simple and improves its flavour.

INGREDIENTS

200g TOMATO KETCHUP

1 TBSP SWEET SMOKED PAPRIKA

1½ TSP CASTER SUGAR

1 TBSP WHITE WINE VINEGAR

¼ TSP GARLIC POWDER

METHOD

1. Mix all the ingredients and beat with a balloon whisk until combined. You want to ensure that there are no lumps of paprika or garlic powder.

2. Use immediately or refrigerate in an airtight container for up to 1 week.

Tomato Salsa

SERVES 4–6

As well as a piquant dip for tortilla chips,
this makes a fine companion to grilled meat and fish.

INGREDIENTS

700g MEDIUM TOMATOES (ABOUT 10 IN TOTAL)

1 SMALL RED ONION, PEELED AND VERY FINELY DICED

2 LONG RED CHILLIES, SEEDED AND VERY FINELY CHOPPED

JUICE OF 2 LIMES

1 TSP SEA SALT

A COUPLE OF HANDFULS OF CORIANDER LEAVES, CHOPPED

METHOD

1. Quarter the tomatoes, cutting away any bits of stalk, then discard the seeds and excess juice from 6 of them. This will help ensure that your salsa isn't too watery.

2. Finely dice all the tomatoes and place in a medium mixing bowl.

3. Add the onion, chillies, lime juice and salt and mix until everything is combined.

4. Add the coriander, gently mix again and taste, adding a little more salt if necessary.

5. Use immediately or refrigerate in an airtight container for up to 2 days. If you leave the salsa longer than a few hours, you may find you need to drain off a little bit of liquid – this is normal.

Tomato Relish

MAKES ENOUGH FOR 4–6 HAMBURGERS

Fresh and zingy, not vinegary and sharp
like so many of its off-the-shelf alternatives.

INGREDIENTS

40g BUTTER

2 LARGE GARLIC CLOVES, PEELED AND SLICED

¼ LONG RED CHILLI, SLICED

200g CANNED CHOPPED TOMATOES

15g CASTER SUGAR

1 TSP ONION POWDER

1 TBSP RED WINE VINEGAR

SEA SALT

METHOD

1. Melt the butter in a small saucepan over a medium heat. Add the garlic and chilli and cook for 1–2 minutes until fragrant.

2. Add the rest of the ingredients and mix well. Reduce the heat to medium–low and cover the pan. Simmer gently for 15 minutes, or until slightly thickened.

3. Remove the pan from the heat and leave the relish to cool. Blend in a food processor or blender, or with a stick blender, until completely smooth.

4. Use immediately or refrigerate in an airtight container for up to 1 week.

AÏOLI

*This is one of the most versatile recipes in the book,
and it's great for fries and chips, too.*

INGREDIENTS

4 GARLIC CLOVES, PEELED

1 MEDIUM EGG YOLK, AT ROOM TEMPERATURE

JUICE OF ½ LEMON

2 TSP DIJON MUSTARD

60ML EXTRA VIRGIN OLIVE OIL

140ML OLIVE POMACE, VEGETABLE OR SUNFLOWER OIL

SEA SALT

METHOD

1. Bring a small saucepan of water to the boil. Add the garlic cloves and simmer gently for 5 minutes. Remove with a slotted spoon and transfer to a bowl of iced water. Once cool, remove and pat dry.

2. Put the egg yolk, lemon juice, mustard, a couple of decent pinches of salt and 1 tablespoon water into the bowl of a food processor along with the garlic cloves. Blitz until smooth.

3. Mix the 2 oils in a small jug. With the motor of the food processor running, gradually add the oil in a slow, steady stream. Continue until all the oil is used. Your aïoli should be smooth and glossy.

4. Use immediately or refrigerate in an airtight container for up to 2 days.

BYRON HOT SAUCE

MAKES PLENTY FOR 4 HAMBURGERS

*It's worth sourcing genuine chipotles in adobo rather than
the chipotle pastes and salsas you see in supermarkets.*

INGREDIENTS

175G ROASTED RED PEPPERS – SHOP-BOUGHT AND DRAINED, OR SEE RECIPE ON PAGE 95

3 LONG RED CHILLIES (ABOUT 60G IN TOTAL), SEEDED

1½ TSP CHIPOTLE IN ADOBO

3 TBSP WHITE WINE VINEGAR

4 TSP CASTER SUGAR

½ TSP CAYENNE PEPPER

PINCH OF GARLIC POWDER

METHOD

1. Blend all the ingredients with 2 tablespoons water in a food processor or using a stick blender.

2. Transfer to an airtight container, bottle or jar and refrigerate for up to 1 week.

Blue Cheese Dressing

SERVES 4-6

This recipe is a homage to Fred's mum, who dresses almost every salad she makes with it.

INGREDIENTS

150g BLUE CHEESE, SUCH AS CASHEL BLUE, CRUMBLED

250g MAYONNAISE

120ml BUTTERMILK

2 TSP WHITE WINE VINEGAR

SEA SALT AND FRESHLY GROUND BLACK PEPPER

METHOD

1. Blend two-thirds of the cheese, the mayonnaise, buttermilk, vinegar, a small pinch of salt and a grind of pepper in a food processor or using a stick blender. Taste and adjust the seasoning if necessary.

2. Stir in the remaining cheese, mixing everything gently so you don't break up the cheese too much.

3. Serve the dressing really cold, giving it a good stir to mix everything together. Or transfer it to an airtight container or jar and refrigerate for up to 3 days.

Guacamole

SERVES 4

Fred counts his Mexican sister-in-law's endorsement of his recipe as a true sign of its quality.
She has very high standards.

INGREDIENTS

5 RIPE AVOCADOS, PEELED AND STONED

½ RED PEPPER, SEEDED AND DICED

2 LONG GREEN CHILLIES, SEEDED AND FINELY CHOPPED

1 TOMATO, FINELY CHOPPED

2 SPRING ONIONS, TRIMMED AND FINELY CHOPPED

1 BUNCH OF CORIANDER, LEAVES FINELY CHOPPED

JUICE OF 2 LIMES

1 TSP SEA SALT

METHOD

1. Blend the flesh of 1 of the avocados in a food processor, or using a stick blender. Blend until smooth. Add the flesh of 3 more of the avocados and mash with a fork or potato masher until almost smooth, but still with some texture. Dice the flesh of the last avocado and stir it in.

2. Add the rest of the ingredients and mix gently until everything is combined. The guacamole will keep for up to 2 days in the fridge, but may discolour slightly. It is best eaten on the day it is made.

BYRON SAUCE

MAKES PLENTY FOR 4 HAMBURGERS

Our flagship burger sauce:
simple, appropriate and delicious.

INGREDIENTS

150g MAYONNAISE

75g TOMATO KETCHUP

35g PICKLED GHERKINS, DRAINED

SEA SALT AND FRESHLY GROUND BLACK PEPPER

METHOD

1. In a medium bowl, mix the mayonnaise and ketchup.

2. Very finely chop the drained gherkins and add to the bowl with a pinch of salt and pepper. Mix until everything is evenly distributed. Taste and adjust the seasoning if necessary.

3. Use immediately or refrigerate in an airtight container for up to 1 week.

CHIPOTLE MAYO

MAKES PLENTY FOR 4 HAMBURGERS

Fred created this in 2012 for the Chilli Queen (see page 24) – it would be the sauce on his death-row burger.

INGREDIENTS

90g CHIPOTLE IN ADOBO

170g MAYONNAISE

40g TOMATO KETCHUP

METHOD

1. Blend all the ingredients in a food processor, or using a stick blender, for at least 1 minute until smooth.

2. Transfer the sauce to an airtight container, bottle or jar and refrigerate for up to 1 week.

Byron Spicy BBQ Sauce

MAKES PLENTY FOR 4 HAMBURGERS

With its surprise ingredient of canned peaches, this a benchmark barbecue sauce. In the restaurants we use Atlantic's House of Lords Deluxe Barbeque Sauce, which you can buy online in large quantities. HP Original BBQ Sauce is a good shop-bought alternative. A note on liquid smoke: some brands are stronger than others, so start with 1½ teaspoons and add more if necessary. It, too, is easy to find online.

INGREDIENTS

30g BROWN SUGAR

1cm PIECE OF GINGER, PEELED AND FINELY CHOPPED OR GRATED

½ TSP CHILLI POWDER

2½ TBSP TOMATO KETCHUP

210g BBQ SAUCE

2 TBSP WORCESTERSHIRE SAUCE

2½ TBSP DARK SOY SAUCE

1½ TSP LIQUID SMOKE

2 TBSP WHITE WINE VINEGAR

JUICE OF ½ LEMON

60g DRAINED CANNED PEACHES, ROUGHLY CHOPPED

METHOD

1. Place all the ingredients in a medium saucepan over a medium heat. Bring to the boil, stirring well, then reduce the heat to a gentle simmer and cook for about 10 minutes until the mixture is thick and glossy, stirring occasionally.

2. Remove the pan from the heat and let the sauce cool slightly. Blend the sauce in a blender or food processor until completely smooth and glossy. Leave to cool completely.

3. Once cool, use the sauce immediately or refrigerate in an airtight container for up to 1 week.

Crispy Fried Onions

SERVES 4

We use these in the Roquefort (see page 32) but they go well in lots of hamburgers.

INGREDIENTS

1 MEDIUM RED ONION, PEELED

100g PLAIN FLOUR

SUNFLOWER OR VEGETABLE OIL, FOR DEEP FRYING

METHOD

1. Heat a deep-fat fryer to 180°C (350°F), or pour enough oil into a large, deep saucepan to come one-third of the way up the sides. Heat the oil over a medium heat until it reaches 180°C (350°F). A cooking thermometer is useful but not essential. (A cube of white bread will brown in 40 seconds if the oil is at the right temperature.)

2. While the oil is heating, slice the onion into really thin rings – about 3mm – using a mandoline slicer if you have one. Place them in a medium mixing bowl, making sure all the pieces are separated out into individual rings.

3. Add the flour to a bowl and toss the onion rings through it until every ring is completely coated. Discard any excess flour.

4. Fry the rings in the hot oil for 2–2¼ minutes until crisp and brown. Carefully stir the onions as they cook, using tongs or a slotted spoon, to ensure even cooking. You may need to cook them in 2 batches.

5. Carefully remove the onions with tongs or a slotted spoon and drain in a single layer on kitchen paper. Leave to cool.

PICKLED RED ONIONS

MAKES ENOUGH FOR 4–6 HAMBURGERS

A popular burger garnish in California, with a refreshing acidic crunch.
This keeps well in the fridge.

INGREDIENTS

100ml RED WINE VINEGAR

50g CASTER SUGAR

¼ TSP SEA SALT

1 SMALL RED ONION, PEELED

METHOD

1. Put the vinegar, sugar and salt in a small saucepan over a medium heat. Simmer for 3–4 minutes, stirring now and again until all the sugar and salt have dissolved.

2. Meanwhile, slice the onion into really thin rings – about 2mm – using a mandoline slicer if you have one. Place them in a non-reactive mixing bowl or a suitable jar, making sure all the rings are separated.

3. Pour the hot pickling liquor over the onions and leave to cool. Cover and refrigerate for at least 24 hours for the best results, though you can use them immediately.

QUICK PICKLED CUCUMBERS

SERVES 4–6

INGREDIENTS

1 LONG CUCUMBER, WASHED AND CUT INTO 3–4mm THICK SLICES

1 TSP FINE SEA SALT

100ml WHITE WINE VINEGAR

2 TSP ENGLISH MUSTARD

35g CASTER SUGAR

METHOD

1. Put the cucumber slices in a colander and add the salt, tossing until all the slices are coated. Leave for 20 minutes, then squeeze out as much water as possible.

2. Leave for a further 20 minutes, then squeeze again until all the excess water is removed. Pat the slices dry with kitchen paper.

3. Place the slices in a mixing bowl or suitable jar. Mix the remaining ingredients and pour over the slices.

4. Serve the cucumber immediately or refrigerate in an airtight container for up to 3 days.

PICKLED GHERKINS

MAKES ENOUGH TO FILL A LARGE JAR

*Do have a go at making your own gherkins:
they're simple and delicious.*

INGREDIENTS

250ml WHITE WINE VINEGAR

3 TBSP FINE SEA SALT

75g CASTER SUGAR

1 TBSP YELLOW MUSTARD SEEDS

4 GARLIC CLOVES, PEELED AND THINLY SLICED

25g WHOLE DILL SPRIGS

1kg SMALL MIDDLE-EASTERN CUCUMBERS, WASHED
(OR 3 LONG CUCUMBERS)

METHOD

1. Place the vinegar, salt, sugar and mustard seeds in a medium saucepan with 500ml water. Bring to a simmer, then turn off the heat and stir until the sugar has completely dissolved.

2. Add the garlic and dill and stir into the warm pickling liquor. Set aside to cool.

3. Meanwhile, prepare the cucumbers. Trim the ends off and slice the cucumbers lengthways into quarters or halves depending on their width. If you're using regular cucumbers, trim them and slice them into 3. Slice each length into 6 spears.

4. Place the cucumbers in a sterilised 2L jar and pour over the pickling liquor. Seal the jar and leave for at least 48 hours or up to 1 month. Once opened, store in the fridge.

BREAD & BUTTER PICKLES

MAKES ENOUGH TO FILL A LARGE JAR

*These work well in sandwiches and
are also great for snacking.*

INGREDIENTS

3 LONG CUCUMBERS, WASHED AND CUT INTO 3-4mm THICK SLICES

1 SMALL ONION, PEELED AND CUT INTO 3-4mm THICK SLICES

50g FINE SEA SALT

250ml CIDER VINEGAR

100g LIGHT SOFT BROWN SUGAR

2 TSP GROUND TURMERIC

2 CLOVES

1 TBSP YELLOW MUSTARD SEEDS

1 TSP CELERY SEEDS

METHOD

1. Place the cucumbers and onion in a colander and add the salt, tossing until the vegetables are coated. Leave for 10 minutes, then, in batches, squeeze out as much water as possible.

2. Leave for a further 10 minutes, then squeeze again until all the excess water is removed. Rinse the cucumbers and onion under cold running water to remove some of the saltiness. Squeeze them for a final time and pat dry with kitchen paper.

3. Meanwhile, heat the vinegar, sugar and spices in a medium-large saucepan, stirring until the sugar has dissolved. Bring to a simmer, then add the cucumber and onions. Cook for 2-3 minutes.

4. Remove the pan from the heat. Pour everything into a sterilised 1L jar and seal. Leave for at least 6 hours or up to 3 weeks. Once opened, store in the fridge.

CRISPY SMOKED STREAKY BACON

SERVES 4

INGREDIENTS

12 SLICES OF SMOKED STREAKY BACON

METHOD

1. Preheat the oven to 180°C (350°F).

2. Lay the bacon slices on a large roasting tray in a single layer. Bake for 10 minutes.

3. Remove the tray, flip the bacon slices over and cook for a further 3–4 minutes.

4. When the bacon is crispy (it will get crispier once it's out of the oven) and well coloured, remove from the oven and leave it to cool slightly.

5. Drain the slices of bacon on some kitchen paper to absorb any excess fat. Use immediately or leave to cool completely before storing in an airtight container in the fridge for up to 3 days.

HOMEMADE CHEESE SLICES

MAKES 14–16 SLICES

INGREDIENTS

200ML DOUBLE CREAM

12 SLICES OF AMERICAN CHEESE (240G IN TOTAL)

75G GRATED CHEDDAR CHEESE

90G FINELY GRATED PARMESAN CHEESE

METHOD

1. Heat the cream in a medium saucepan until steaming. Add the American cheese, Cheddar and Parmesan and beat with a fork or balloon whisk over a low heat until the cheese has melted and the sauce is smooth. Do not let the mixture boil.

2. Remove from the heat and pour the mixture onto a large sheet of non-stick parchment paper. Cover with another sheet of the same size. Gently roll out the mixture, using a rolling pin, until 5mm thick.

3. Leave the mixture to cool, then transfer to the fridge on a tray and chill until set.

4. Remove the cheese from the fridge and cut into pieces suitable for hamburgers, cutting through the paper so that each slice is still sandwiched in paper.

5. The cheese slices are now ready use, or you can store them either in the fridge for up to 3 days, or well wrapped in the freezer for up to 1 month.

ROASTED RED PEPPERS

MAKES ENOUGH FOR
4 HAMBURGERS OR MOST SALADS

INGREDIENTS

2 RED PEPPERS

OLIVE OIL

METHOD

1. Preheat the oven to 220°C (425°F).

2. Line a baking tray with foil and place the peppers on it. Drizzle with a little olive oil and rub the oil over the peppers. Roast the peppers in the preheated oven for 20 minutes.

3. After 20 minutes, remove the baking tray from the oven and flip the peppers over. Return to the oven and roast for a further 20 minutes.

4. By now the peppers should be soft and collapsing, with lots of charred areas on the skin. Place the peppers in a heatproof bowl. Cover the bowl with clingfilm to seal in the steam, and leave the peppers to cool slightly.

5. Transfer the peppers to a chopping board. Remove the stalks and peel away the skin. Slice the peppers in half and discard the seeds. Pat dry if necessary.

6. Use the peppers immediately or cover and store in the fridge for up to 3 days.

CRISPY PANCETTA

MAKES 12 SLICES

INGREDIENTS

12 SLICES OF PANCETTA

METHOD

1. Preheat the oven to 180°C (350°F).

2. Place the pancetta slices on a large roasting tray in a single layer. Cook in the preheated oven for 3 minutes. Be careful, as pancetta can burn swiftly.

3. When the pancetta is crisp (it will get crispier once it's out of the oven) and well coloured, remove from the oven and leave to cool slightly.

4. Drain the slices of pancetta on kitchen paper to absorb excess fat. Use immediately or cool completely before storing in an airtight container in the fridge for up to 3 days.

Welsh Rarebit

MAKES ENOUGH FOR 4 HAMBURGERS

INGREDIENTS

80ML PALE ALE

2 TBSP WORCESTERSHIRE SAUCE

2 TBSP ENGLISH MUSTARD

75ML DOUBLE CREAM

1 TSP BYRON HOT SAUCE (SEE PAGE 84), OR YOUR FAVOURITE HOT SAUCE (NOT TABASCO)

20G CORNFLOUR

2 TBSP WHOLE MILK

50G GRATED PARMESAN CHEESE

260G GRATED CHEDDAR CHEESE

METHOD

1. Put the ale, Worcestershire sauce, mustard, cream and Byron Hot Sauce in a saucepan over a medium heat and bring to a gentle simmer.

2. Meanwhile, mix the cornflour and milk together into a thin paste.

3. When the liquid in the saucepan is simmering, add the cornflour mixture and the Parmesan. Whisk over a medium-low heat until the mixture is smooth and thickened and the Parmesan has melted, about 4–5 minutes. Remove from the heat and leave to cool.

4. When cool, stir in the Cheddar. Shape the mixture into balls weighing 30g each. Place them, one by one, between 2 pieces of parchment paper and flatten until about 10cm wide. Refrigerate until ready to use. It will keep in an airtight container for up to 1 week. It's great melted onto toast.

Buttered Onions

MAKES ENOUGH FOR 4 HAMBURGERS

INGREDIENTS

1 WHITE ONION, ROUGHLY CHOPPED

50G UNSALTED BUTTER

¼ TSP SEA SALT

½ TSP CASTER SUGAR

METHOD

1. Blitz the onion in a food processor until extremely finely chopped, or very finely chop it using a knife.

2. Put a saucepan of water over a medium heat and bring to the boil. Tip the onion into the boiling water and simmer gently for 3 minutes. Drain in a sieve or colander, pushing the onion against the base of the sieve or colander to remove as much liquid as possible.

3. Dry out the pan you had been boiling the onion in and melt the butter in it over a medium heat. Add the onion with the salt and sugar. Reduce the heat to medium-low and cook gently, stirring now and again, for 20 minutes until the onion has absorbed all the butter and is beautifully soft, but not browned. Leave to cool before using.

CRISPY POTATOES

MAKES ENOUGH FOR 4 HAMBURGERS

INGREDIENTS

2 MEDIUM MARIS PIPER POTATOES, WASHED

VEGETABLE OR SUNFLOWER OIL,
FOR DEEP FRYING

SEA SALT

METHOD

1. Finely grate the washed potatoes. Rinse under a cold tap for up to 5 minutes, or until the water runs clear. Drain them.

2. Set the drained potatoes aside for at least 5 minutes. Finally, pat them dry with kitchen paper.

3. Heat a deep-fat fryer to 180°C (350°F), or pour enough oil into a large, deep saucepan to come one-third of the way up the sides. Heat the oil over a medium heat until it reaches 180°C (350°F). A cooking thermometer is useful but not essential. (A cube of white bread will brown in 40 seconds if the oil is at the right temperature.)

4. Carefully drop the potatoes into the hot oil in small batches. Use tongs or a slotted spoon to carefully move the potatoes around. Fry for about 2–2½ minutes until crisp and golden. When the oil stops sizzling, the potatoes should be ready.

5. Carefully remove the crispy potatoes from the oil and drain well on kitchen paper. Season with a little sea salt.

CHAPTER 4

Food To Share

No doubt you've had average versions of ribs, buffalo wings and mozzarella sticks before, but these recipes restore the magic of these dishes. A homemade pork scratching is a completely different beast from something that comes in a packet, and properly done nachos are a wonder.

This is food to get people round for – for a Fourth of July or Halloween party – as the keynotes of a summer barbecue or during an indulgent night in with friends.

Fred always does the honey-glazed dogs at his family Christmas bash: last year, 450 of them vanished in minutes.

A few rolls of kitchen paper will come in handy – these are the most tactile, informal and probably the messiest dishes in this book. But therein lies the secret. This is properly sociable food. You know you like the people you're eating with when the sticky BBQ ribs have smeared sauce on your chin – and nobody cares.

Buffalo Chicken Wings

SERVES 4

The aim is to get a glass-like surface on the wings, so that they are completely covered in that shiny, sticky coating.

INGREDIENTS

1kg CHICKEN WINGS, TIPS REMOVED, WINGS SEPARATED AT THEIR JOINTS INTO 2 PIECES

100g RICE FLOUR

RANCH DRESSING (SEE PAGE 82) OR BLUE CHEESE DRESSING (SEE PAGE 85), TO SERVE (OPTIONAL)

VEGETABLE, SUNFLOWER OR GROUNDNUT OIL, FOR DEEP FRYING

For the hot-sauce glaze

200ml BYRON HOT SAUCE (SEE PAGE 84), OR YOUR FAVOURITE HOT SAUCE, E.G. FRANK'S OR CHOLULA (NOT TABASCO)

1 TSP CORNFLOUR

2 TBSP WHITE WINE VINEGAR

30g UNSALTED BUTTER, CUBED

METHOD

1. For the hot-sauce glaze, whisk together 1 tablespoon of the Byron Hot Sauce and the cornflour in a small bowl until completely smooth.

2. Pour the rest of the hot sauce, and the vinegar, into a small saucepan over a medium heat. Beat in the cornflour mixture with a balloon whisk until combined.

3. Stir in the butter, mixing until it has melted. Remove the pan from the heat, leave to cool slightly, then blend using a blender or food processor until completely incorporated and lightened in colour. Leave to cool.

4. Heat a deep-fat fryer to 190°C (375°F), or pour enough oil into a large, deep saucepan to come one-third of the way up the sides. Heat the oil over a medium heat until it reaches 190°C (375°F). A cooking thermometer is useful but not essential. (A cube of white bread will brown in 30 seconds if the oil is at the right temperature.)

5. Toss the chicken wings in the rice flour in a shallow bowl until completely coated. As you toss, bash the wings about a little to try to get the rice flour into the "hinges" of each wing. Shake off any excess flour.

6. Cook the wings in the hot oil, in batches, for 8 minutes, or until cooked through. Be sure not to overcrowd the pan, if using, as this will reduce the temperature of the oil and cause the wings to become greasy. Carefully remove the cooked wings with a slotted spoon and set aside to drain on kitchen paper for a minute or so.

7. Add some of the glaze to a large mixing bowl, then drop in a few of the cooked wings and toss until well coated. Repeat the process with the remaining wings.

8. Serve immediately. These are delicious with either Ranch Dressing or Blue Cheese Dressing on the side.

Nachos

Granted, they're a little trashy, but made properly these remind you why nachos became so popular in the first place. If you want to make your own tortilla chips, cut shop-bought tortilla wraps into eight wedges, drizzle with oil and bake in a 180 °C (350 °F) oven for 8–10 minutes until crisp.

INGREDIENTS

250g TORTILLA CHIPS

200g GRATED MONTEREY JACK CHEESE

75-100g SLICED JALAPEÑOS, TO TASTE (OPTIONAL)

TOMATO SALSA (SEE PAGE 83)

GUACAMOLE (SEE PAGE 85)

90ml SOUR CREAM

A HANDFUL OF CORIANDER LEAVES, ROUGHLY CHOPPED

METHOD

1 Preheat the oven to 200 °C (400 °F).

2. Place half the tortilla chips in a medium ovenproof dish. Sprinkle over half the grated cheese, then top with the rest of the tortilla chips. Scatter over the jalapeños, if using, then add the remaining cheese.

3. Bake in the preheated oven for 7–10 minutes until the cheese is completely melted and gooey. Keep an eye on the dish, as the tortilla chips can burn easily – as soon as the cheese has melted, remove the dish from the oven.

4. Dot the Tomato Salsa, Guacamole and sour cream over the top of the tortilla chips, pushing some down into the lower layers. Scatter with the coriander leaves and eat immediately.

Chicken Nuggets

SERVES 4

Perfect finger food, and great for kids.
No weird chemicals or processed meat here: just good-quality chicken, cooked with care.

INGREDIENTS

3 SKINLESS CHICKEN BREASTS

200ml BUTTERMILK

¼ TSP ONION POWDER

¼ TSP GARLIC POWDER

150g PANKO BREADCRUMBS

SUNFLOWER, VEGETABLE OR GROUNDNUT OIL, FOR SHALLOW FRYING

FINE SEA SALT AND FRESHLY GROUND BLACK PEPPER

METHOD

1. Remove the fillets from the breasts (if still attached). Slice the fillets in half and then slice the breasts into 4 or 5 similarly sized pieces.

2. In a large bowl, beat the buttermilk, onion and garlic powders with a fork or balloon whisk, ensuring there are no lumps. Season with salt and pepper, using as little or as much as you and your children like.

3. Add the chicken pieces to the batter and mix. At this point, you can cover the bowl and leave the chicken in the fridge to marinate for up to 12 hours if desired.

4. Place the panko breadcrumbs in a large bowl. Fill a large, deep frying pan with 1.5cm oil and get a large plate ready, lined with a couple of sheets of kitchen paper. Heat the oil over a medium-high heat – a piece of breadcrumb dropped into the oil should sizzle.

5. Take the pieces of chicken out of the buttermilk batter one by one and turn in the bowl of breadcrumbs until covered. Transfer the pieces to a plate or tray. Repeat with the remaining pieces of chicken.

6. Cook the chicken pieces in the hot oil, in batches, for 2–3 minutes. Flip them over with tongs and cook for a further 2–3 minutes on the other side, until the breadcrumbs are dark gold and the chicken is cooked through. If they are browning too quickly, turn down the heat slightly.

7. Remove the nuggets from the oil with a slotted spoon and leave to drain on kitchen paper. Serve with a dip of your choice.

Jasper Cuppaidge and I go back a long way. Little did we know, when we were both working in London's pubs and restaurants in our younger days, that he would become the founder of Camden Town Brewery, while I would have a clutch of hamburger joints on my hands. Things worked out pretty well, though, because when it came to putting together a top-notch craft beer list for Byron, Jasper was exactly the person I needed. He suggested a trip to San Diego's annual beer festival to get a taste of the scene.

We were reminiscing about the past over a beer when a friendly voice interrupted. "Hey – you're English?" I was, I said, as a convivial hand extended to shake mine. "That's awesome! Having a good time here?" I was. "What do you know - we've just started selling our beer to a guy with a bunch of hamburger joints in London!" Oh really? I said. What's his name? "Oh... I don't know. Tom something?"

The guys from Ska Brewing in Colorado make some of my favourite beers, and now, by happy coincidence, they became our unofficial chaperones around San Diego. The memories of the rest of that night may be a little hazy, but it seems nobody disgraced themselves too much, because we're still serving their brilliant beers to this day.

Honey-Glazed "Dogs"

SERVES 6-8

Perhaps the simplest recipe in this book, but one of the most delicious.

INGREDIENTS

60 COCKTAIL/MINI SAUSAGES, APPROX. 850g

SUNFLOWER, VEGETABLE OR OLIVE OIL

175g RUNNY HONEY

85g WHOLEGRAIN MUSTARD

20g DIJON MUSTARD

1 TSP DARK SOY SAUCE

1 TSP BALSAMIC VINEGAR

METHOD

1. Preheat the oven to 190°C (375°F).

2. Spread the sausages on a large baking tray and add a splash of cooking oil. Roll the sausages in the oil to coat. Roast for 10-15 minutes until lightly coloured and cooked through.

3. Meanwhile, stir the remaining ingredients together in a small saucepan over a medium heat. Keep the sauce warm until the sausages are cooked.

4. Remove the sausages from the oven, pouring away most of the fat.

5. Pour the warm sauce over the sausages, turning until evenly covered. Return to the oven for a further 3 minutes to ensure the sauce sticks properly to the sausages.

6. Remove the sausages from the oven and leave to cool slightly before serving.

Mozzarella Sticks

If you've only tried the industrial, factory-made versions of mozzarella sticks, you may be wondering why we've included them in the book. Do give them a go: the ones that come in packets are travesties of the real thing. These are delicious dipped in Tomato Relish (see page 83).

INGREDIENTS

2 BALLS OF MOZZARELLA, DRAINED

2 SPRIGS OF THYME, LEAVES ONLY

100g PLAIN FLOUR

3 MEDIUM EGGS, LIGHTLY BEATEN

250g PANKO BREADCRUMBS

A DASH OF WHOLE MILK

SUNFLOWER, VEGETABLE OR GROUNDNUT OIL, FOR SHALLOW FRYING

SEA SALT AND FRESHLY GROUND BLACK PEPPER

METHOD

1. Slice the mozzarella and then cut each piece in half. Spread the slices out on a plate or tray and season with a little salt and pepper. Scatter over the thyme leaves and set aside.

2. Place the flour, eggs and breadcrumbs in 3 wide, shallow bowls. Add a dash of milk to the beaten eggs and mix.

3. Dip each mozzarella stick in the flour until evenly coated and shake off any excess. Next, dip each mozzarella stick into the egg, coating well and allowing any excess egg to drip off. Finally, turn each mozzarella stick in the breadcrumbs until completely covered. Repeat with the remaining sticks.

4. Now dip each mozzarella stick in the egg again, and then return them to the breadcrumbs so that each has a second layer. This will help seal the mozzarella and prevent it from running.

5. Place the sticks in a single layer on a tray or large plate. Cover and freeze for 1–2 hours to firm them up.

6. When ready to cook, fill a large, deep frying pan with 1cm oil. Heat until a piece of breadcrumb dropped in the oil sizzles.

7. Fry the mozzarella sticks, in batches, for 2–4 minutes, flipping with tongs until golden all over and melting in the middle.

8. Lift the mozzarella sticks from the oil with a slotted spoon and drain on kitchen paper. Serve warm with a dip of your choice.

Sticky BBQ Ribs

SERVES 4

Rib meat, falling from the bone and slathered in barbecue sauce, is one of the enduring tastes of the South. Make sure you have a stack of napkins on hand.

INGREDIENTS

2 RACKS OF BABY BACK RIBS (1.5–2kg IN TOTAL), WITH THE MEMBRANE REMOVED (ASK YOUR BUTCHER)

1 QUANTITY OF BYRON SPICY BBQ SAUCE (SEE PAGE 89)

METHOD

1. Preheat the oven to 150°C (300°F).

2. Preheat a BBQ or griddle pan until hot. Once hot, place the ribs on the BBQ or griddle and cook on both sides, turning now and again, until charred and caramelised.

3. Place the ribs on a large roasting tray and run the Byron Spicy BBQ Sauce all over them.

4. Cover the tray tightly with foil and place in the oven. Bake for 2 hours until tender, turning the ribs now and again and basting with any juices in the bottom of the tray.

5. Remove the cooked ribs from the oven and leave until cool enough to handle. Place on a chopping board, keeping any excess sauce.

6. Separate the meat into individual ribs, brush with the leftover sauce and serve immediately.

Pork Scratchings

SERVES 4

As well as being great with drinks, these go beautifully alongside the Miami Slice burger (see page 30) – where they would properly be known as chicharrónes.

INGREDIENTS

1 PIECE OF PORK SKIN WITH 1cm FAT ATTACHED, APPROX. 20 X 12cm

FINE SEA SALT

SUNFLOWER OR VEGETABLE OIL, FOR ROASTING

METHOD

1. Preheat the oven to 220°C (425°F).

2. With a sharp knife, slice the pork skin widthways into 1cm thick strips.

3. Season the strips generously with salt and set aside for 20 minutes.

4. Place the pork strips on a baking tray and drizzle 1 tablespoon oil over them. Roast in the preheated oven for 15 minutes.

5. Reduce the oven temperature to 180°C (350°F) and cook for a further 20–25 minutes until the pork is crispy but still slightly soft. Remove from the oven and leave to cool.

WHOLEY COW

How many hamburgers can you make out of one cow? It's something we'd often wondered, but we'd never really tried to find out – until one weekend in August, when we threw a party we called "Wholey Cow".

Fred had long wanted to prove just what we could do with a single cow – to do justice to the animal by using as much of it as possible, and by being part of the process almost from start to finish. We travelled to Scotland, found our beast, went with it to the abattoir, and finally, Fred butchered it just the way he wanted it, dividing up the cuts that could be ground into hamburgers, those that would need slower cooking in a rich beef chilli, and those we would cure to make "beef bacon".

There's an honesty, however brutal, in witnessing exactly what it takes to get your meat from field to fork. Even the bones went into making stock for my tried-and-tested recipe for Bloody Bull cocktails (imagine a Bloody Mary, but with added beef consommé – see page 178).

We invited a few hundred of our closest friends and regular customers, pitched up our van in the grounds of Camden Town Brewery, fired up the grills, and got serving. Two days later, all that remained of our cow were a few portions of chilli and a lot of satisfied punters.

And the answer? About 900 hamburgers, give or take.

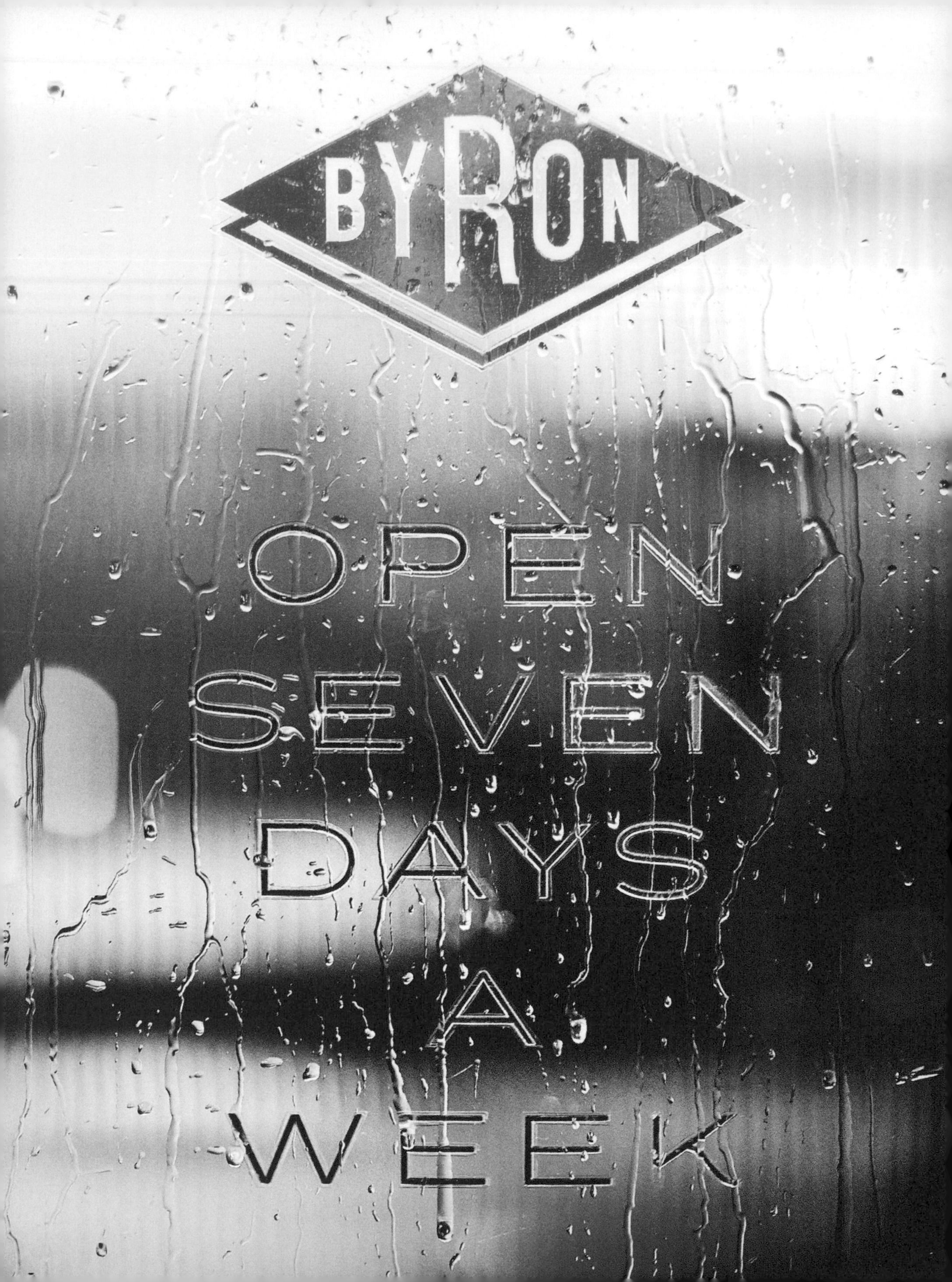
BYRON
OPEN
SEVEN
DAYS
A
WEEK

CHAPTER 5

WHEN IT'S RAINED OFF

Sometimes you crave food to hunker down with. These recipes will meet that need. Eat them when the weather is howling and, as the title suggests, the match is cancelled – or just when it's a bit blustery and your brisk afternoon walk is seeming less and less inviting.

You'll find a "more is more" approach is best when eating this kind of food: triple grilled cheese would never have emerged in a parsimonious British kitchen, and a good club sandwich should always feel generous, maybe even a little excessive.

The inspiration for these dishes comes from America, of course, but some of them are becoming classics in British kitchens as well. Chilli, meatballs and even short rib are appearing increasingly regularly on our country's tables, thanks partly to chefs who have enjoyed them in the States and brought them home. But Fred's recipes show them at their best.

MEATLOAF

SERVES 6–8

Meatloaf has rather fallen from fashion these days, which is a shame.
It's economical, hearty cooking that can feed a lot of people; the key is not to overcook it.
This one has big hits of flavour from the blue cheese running through it and its generous ketchup glaze.
You will need a large loaf tin for this recipe.

INGREDIENTS

10g UNSALTED BUTTER

8 SLICES OF SMOKED STREAKY BACON, FINELY CHOPPED

3 STICKS OF CELERY, FINELY DICED

2 ONIONS, FINELY DICED

1 RED PEPPER, SEEDED AND FINELY DICED

4 GARLIC CLOVES, FINELY CHOPPED

750g MINCED BEEF

250g SAUSAGEMEAT

3 TBSP WORCESTERSHIRE SAUCE

1 BUNCH OF PARSLEY (APPROX. 40g), LEAVES ONLY, FINELY CHOPPED

150g FRESH WHITE BREADCRUMBS

4 MEDIUM EGGS

150g TOMATO KETCHUP

90g ROQUEFORT CHEESE, SLICED

SEA SALT AND FRESHLY GROUND BLACK PEPPER

METHOD

1. Melt the butter in a medium saucepan, then fry the chopped bacon until crisp.

2. Add the celery, onions, pepper and a pinch of salt and stir. Cover and cook for 15 minutes or until completely soft, adding the garlic for the final 2 minutes. Remove the pan from the heat and leave to cool a little.

3. Preheat the oven to 160°C (325°F).

4. Put the beef, sausagemeat, Worcestershire sauce, parsley, breadcrumbs, eggs and one-third of the ketchup in a large mixing bowl. Tip in the vegetables and bacon. Mix well.

5. Fry a small patty of the mixture in a frying pan for a couple of minutes on each side until cooked through. Check the seasoning.

6. Spread another third of the ketchup in the bottom of a 900g loaf tin so it covers the base. Add one-third of the meat mixture and spread it out evenly. Top with the sliced cheese.

7. Add the remaining meat mixture and press down gently to form into a dome shape. Spread the remaining ketchup over the top of the meat, then cover the meatloaf tightly with foil, tucking the edges under the rim of the loaf tin. Place the pan on a roasting tray. Bake for 1 hour and 15 minutes.

8. Rest the meatloaf for 15 minutes, then gently turn it out of the loaf tin and place onto a board. Serve in slices. This is delicious with a fried egg and French fries!

MEATBALLS

SERVES 4

*We love meatballs, one of the great Italian-American creations, famously celebrated in
Martin Scorsese's gangster classic,* Goodfellas. *Soaking the breadcrumbs in milk gives them a wonderful soft texture.
These go well with spaghetti, but try them stuffed in a baguette as well.*

INGREDIENTS

For the meatballs

2 TBSP OLIVE OIL

1 MEDIUM RED ONION, FINELY DICED

3 SMALL SPRIGS OF THYME, LEAVES ONLY, CHOPPED

1 LARGE GARLIC CLOVE, FINELY CHOPPED

30G FRESH WHITE BREADCRUMBS

100ML WHOLE MILK

250G MINCED BEEF

250G MINCED PORK

30G FINELY GRATED PARMESAN

½ BUNCH OF PARSLEY, LEAVES ONLY, FINELY CHOPPED

1 MEDIUM EGG, LIGHTLY BEATEN

GRATED ZEST OF ½ LEMON

SEA SALT AND FRESHLY GROUND BLACK PEPPER

For the tomato sauce

3 TBSP OLIVE OIL

3 GARLIC CLOVES, CHOPPED

PINCH OF DRIED CHILLI FLAKES (OPTIONAL)

400G CAN CHOPPED TOMATOES

ABOUT ¼ TSP CASTER SUGAR

¼ TSP RED WINE VINEGAR

2 LARGE SPRIGS OF BASIL, 1 WHOLE, 1 LEAVES ONLY, SHREDDED

METHOD

1. For the meatballs, heat half the olive oil in a medium frying pan over a medium heat. Add the onion and a pinch of salt, cover and sweat the onion for 12–15 minutes or until completely soft and translucent. Add the thyme leaves halfway through.

2. When the onion is soft, add the garlic and cook over a low heat, uncovered, for 3 minutes, or until softened. Remove the pan from the heat.

3. Soak the breadcrumbs in the milk until softened.

4. For the tomato sauce, heat the olive oil in a medium–large saucepan over a medium heat. Add the garlic and chilli flakes, if using, and stir in the oil for 15 seconds, then pour in the canned tomatoes.

5. Season the tomato sauce with 1 teaspoon salt, the sugar, vinegar and the whole basil sprig. Add 75ml water (you can wash the tomato can out with this if you like). Bring the pan to the boil, reduce the heat and simmer gently for 25–30 minutes or until thickened. Taste and adjust the seasoning. You can add another little pinch of sugar if necessary. Remove from the heat.

6. In a large mixing bowl, mix the minced beef and pork, Parmesan, parsley, egg, lemon zest and breadcrumbs. Season generously with pepper and add the cooled onion mixture. Mix well.

7. Divide the meatball mixture into 12 portions and roll into neat balls.

8. Heat the remaining olive oil in a large, heavy-based frying pan over a medium heat. Add the meatballs and cook, turning now and again, until browned on all sides. Meanwhile, reheat the tomato sauce gently over a medium–low heat.

9. When the meatballs are browned, add them to the hot sauce and simmer gently for 10 minutes to cook through. Add the shredded basil leaves, stir through and continue cooking for a further 5 minutes. Serve with spaghetti or in Meatball Sandwiches (see page 130).

BRAISED SHORT RIBS

SERVES 4

This dish, a kind of American bœuf bourguignon, is ideal for a dinner party as it reheats well.
Short ribs contain a lot of fat: slow-cooking them brings them a terrific melting texture.

INGREDIENTS

4 BEEF SHORT RIBS (APPROX. 400–500G EACH), TRIMMED

2 X 250G PIECES OF SMOKED BACON OR PANCETTA

3 CARROTS, PEELED AND QUARTERED

2 ONIONS, HALVED

2 STICKS OF CELERY, ROUGHLY CHOPPED

1 WHOLE STAR ANISE

1 WHOLE GARLIC BULB, SLICED THROUGH THE MIDDLE

½ BUNCH OF THYME (ABOUT 8G)

2 TBSP WORCESTERSHIRE SAUCE

1 BOTTLE OF FULL-BODIED RED WINE, E.G. MERLOT

1L GOOD-QUALITY BEEF STOCK

METHOD

1. Heat a very large saucepan or cast-iron pot over a high heat. When hot, add the short ribs, fat side down, along with just one of the pieces of smoked bacon or pancetta. Brown the meat on all sides. Depending on the size of your pan, you may need to do this in batches, transferring the browned pieces of meat to a plate while you cook the remaining pieces.

2. When all of the meat is browned, remove from the pan. Tip in the carrots, onions, celery and star anise and stir around to cook in the fat left over from the meat. Scrape up any bits stuck to the bottom of the pan. Continue to cook for 3–4 minutes or until the vegetables are lightly browned.

3. Add the garlic, thyme and Worcestershire sauce and mix into the vegetables. Pour in the red wine and bring to the boil. Continue to boil until reduced by three-quarters. This can take up to 25 minutes, depending on the size of your pan.

4. Now pour in the stock, stir well, then return the short ribs and bacon to the pan along with any juices that have collected on the plate.

5. Bring the pan to the boil and, reduce to a very gentle simmer over a low heat. Cover and cook for 4 hours, or until the meat is tender and falling off the bone.

6. When the ribs are ready, remove them from the sauce and strain the sauce through a colander into a large bowl. Discard the contents of the colander and pour the drained liquid back into the saucepan. Skim off and discard any excess fat, and bring the pan to the boil over a medium–high heat. Boil until reduced by half.

7. Pull the bones out of the short ribs and remove any sinew or gristle from the outside of the meat, then place the meat back into the reduced sauce to warm through over a medium heat.

8. Finely dice the remaining bacon or pancetta and fry in a small pan until crisp. Drain off any excess oil and tip the bacon or pancetta into the reduced sauce, mixing it in.

9. Serve the hot short ribs, one per person, on a plate with the sauce spooned over the top. They go well with mashed potato.

BEEF CHILLI

SERVES 6

Cooking with whole shin rather than minced beef leads to an incomparably better dish. The mixture will have a lot of chilli heat at the start, but don't worry: it mellows over time. If you're using a stock cube, don't season the dish until the end, when everything will have reduced. To make this into a filling, one-pot meal, add a couple of cans of drained, rinsed kidney beans before you add the coriander and warm them through. With rice, sour cream, some grated cheese and a few bowls of Guacamole (see page 85) and Tomato Salsa (see page 83), you've got a feast.

INGREDIENTS

2.5KG BEEF SHIN, CUT ACROSS THE BONE, OSSO BUCCO-STYLE, INTO 6 OR 7 PIECES

2 ONIONS, ROUGHLY CHOPPED

3 CARROTS, PEELED AND ROUGHLY CHOPPED

1 GREEN PEPPER, SEEDED AND ROUGHLY CHOPPED

3 LONG GREEN CHILLIES, ROUGHLY CHOPPED

100ML RED WINE VINEGAR

2L BEEF STOCK

3 WHOLE DRIED GUAJILLO CHILLIES

4 WHOLE DRIED CHIPOTLE CHILLIES

3 WHOLE DRIED ARBOL CHILLIES

350G ROASTED RED PEPPERS - SHOP-BOUGHT AND DRAINED, OR SEE RECIPE ON PAGE 95 - FINELY CHOPPED

½ TSP SWEET SMOKED PAPRIKA

OLIVE OIL, FOR FRYING

SEA SALT AND FRESHLY GROUND BLACK PEPPER

CORIANDER LEAVES, TO SERVE

METHOD

1. Heat a very large saucepan or cast-iron pot over a high heat and add a dash of olive oil. Add the beef shin and brown on all sides. Depending on the size of your pan, you may need to do this in batches.

2. Remove the meat from the pan. Tip the vegetables and green chillies into the pan. Cook for 4–6 minutes over a high heat until lightly caramelised.

3. Pour the vinegar into the pan and, using a wooden spoon, scrape the bottom to dislodge any lovely sticky bits from the meat and vegetables. Let the vinegar bubble up for a minute or two over the high heat.

4. Pour in the stock, return the meat to the pan, add the whole dried chillies and bring to a simmer. Now reduce the heat to low, cover and leave to simmer very gently for 4 hours or until the meat is falling off the bone.

5. When the meat is ready, remove it from the sauce and pour this through a colander into a large bowl. Discard the contents of the colander and pour the drained liquid back into the saucepan. Boil over a high heat until reduced by about half.

6. Meanwhile, remove the bones and any gristle from the shin, making sure to keep any bone marrow (simply push the marrow out of the bones). Roughly mash the meat with a wooden spoon. The meat should fall apart easily. Discard any gristle. When all the meat is shredded and the liquid reduced by half, return the meat to the liquid along with the finely chopped roasted red peppers. Mix well.

7. Bring the liquid back to the boil, then reduce to a simmer. Stir in the sweet smoked paprika, mixing well so that it is evenly distributed. Season to taste. Serve the chilli, once heated through, with some coriander leaves sprinkled over the top.

FRIED CHICKEN

SERVES 4

Fred recently went on a three-day "chicken pilgrimage" to Dallas, Texas, where some of the best fried chicken comes from. He commandeered a driver to take him round endless chicken joints – perfect for propagating the myth of the eccentric Englishman. This is the result: a Southern-style batter holding tender meat. Ideally, start marinating the chicken in the morning to cook it in the evening. But if you need to use it straightaway, that's fine.

INGREDIENTS

VEGETABLE OIL, FOR DEEP FRYING

For the marinade

600ml BUTTERMILK

2 TSP FINE SEA SALT

1 TSP ONION POWDER

½ TSP GARLIC POWDER

½ TSP SWEET SMOKED PAPRIKA

4 CHICKEN THIGHS, SKIN ON

4 CHICKEN DRUMSTICKS, SKIN ON

For the spiced flour

1 TSP ONION POWDER

½ TSP GARLIC POWDER

1 TSP SWEET SMOKED PAPRIKA

1 TSP GROUND WHITE PEPPER

1 TSP GROUND BLACK PEPPER

1 TSP MUSTARD POWDER

3 TSP FINE SEA SALT

200g PLAIN FLOUR

50g WHITE RICE FLOUR

METHOD

1. For the marinade, whisk together the buttermilk, salt, onion and garlic powders, and paprika in a mixing bowl with a fork or balloon whisk. Make sure there are no lumps. Add the chicken and stir to coat. Cover and leave to marinate in the fridge for up to 48 hours (see Introduction above).

2. For the spiced flour, whisk all the ingredients well in a large mixing bowl.

3. When ready to cook the chicken, heat a deep-fat fryer to 160°C (325°F), or pour enough oil into a large, deep saucepan to come one-third of the way up the sides. Heat the oil over a medium heat until it reaches 160°C (325°F). A cooking thermometer is useful but not essential. (A cube of white bread will brown in 60 seconds if the oil is at the right temperature.)

4. While the oil is heating, remove the chicken pieces from the marinade, shaking off all but a little of the excess buttermilk. Toss in the spiced flour, making sure each piece of chicken is covered.

5. Cook the chicken pieces in the hot oil, in batches, for 15–16 minutes until golden and cooked through. Every time you add new pieces of chicken, the temperature of the oil will drop. Try to maintain the temperature between 150°C (300°F) and 160°C (325°F) throughout the cooking process by adjusting the temperature of the heat below the oil.

6. Remove each cooked piece of chicken carefully with a slotted spoon or "spider", drain briefly on kitchen paper and serve immediately.

ALTERNATIVE METHOD

Prepare the recipe up to the end of Step 2. Place a large, deep frying pan over a medium heat. Add enough vegetable oil to come 1cm up the sides of the pan. Carefully place the chicken pieces in the oil and cook, turning frequently, for 20–25 minutes until the chicken is ready. To avoid overcrowding, you may find it easier to use 2 separate frying pans, or to fry in batches.

This is the way fried chicken is traditionally prepared. Use lard as the cooking oil for an amazing result.

PHILLY CHEESESTEAK

SERVES 2

One of the iconic roadside foods of America: a long roll stuffed with chopped, flash-fried steak, caramelised onions and melted cheese. Traditionally, this is made with roast beef, and if you have some left over, it's a great way of using it up. If you can't find provolone cheese and don't have any Homemade Cheese Slices to hand, then a mixture of mozzarella and Cheddar will give you a good, stringy cheese with a decent mature taste.

INGREDIENTS

OLIVE OIL, FOR FRYING

1 LARGE ONION, PEELED AND SLICED

1 GREEN PEPPER, SEEDED AND SLICED

2 SUB ROLLS, HALVED

1 RUMP STEAK (APPROX. 250-300g), TRIMMED OF ANY FAT AND SINEW

8 HOMEMADE CHEESE SLICES (SEE PAGE 94), OR 8 SLICES OF PROVOLONE CHEESE (ALTERNATIVELY, USE THIN SLICES OF CHEDDAR [50g IN TOTAL] UNDERNEATH ½ BALL SLICED MOZZARELLA)

SEA SALT

METHOD

1. Heat a splash of olive oil in a medium saucepan over a medium heat. Add the onion and a pinch of salt, cover and sweat for 4–5 minutes until softened slightly.

2. Preheat the grill to high.

3. Add the pepper to the onion, cover and cook for a further 12–14 minutes until the onion has completely softened and the pepper is cooked.

4. Lightly toast or grill the cut sides of the sub rolls.

5. Cut the steak into wafer-thin slices. Heat another dash of oil in a large frying pan over a medium heat. Fry the steak for 1 minute, or until lightly browned, stirring frequently.

6. Add the seared steak slices to the pan of vegetables and cook for a further 15 seconds.

7. Add your chosen cheese slices to the pan on top of everything else and cook for 1½–2 minutes until the cheese has melted.

8. Divide the mixture between the toasted rolls, sandwich together and serve immediately.

SLOPPY JOE

SERVES 4

An approachable dish, but perhaps one to serve to best friends and not when you're on a first date.
The minced beef has a whack of umami from all the tomato, Worcestershire sauce and Tabasco;
it works well with an inauthentic slice of grilled cheese.

INGREDIENTS

25g UNSALTED BUTTER

2 MEDIUM ONIONS, VERY THINLY SLICED

2 GARLIC CLOVES, FINELY CHOPPED

450g MINCED BEEF

2 TBSP WORCESTERSHIRE SAUCE

1 TSP TABASCO SAUCE, OR TO TASTE

110g TOMATO PURÉE

2 TBSP TOMATO KETCHUP

2 ROASTED RED PEPPERS – SHOP-BOUGHT
AND DRAINED, OR SEE RECIPE ON PAGE 95
– FINELY CHOPPED

4 BUNS, HALVED

FINE SEA SALT AND FRESHLY GROUND
BLACK PEPPER

METHOD

1. Melt the butter in a medium saucepan over a high heat. Fry the onions for 8 minutes or until lightly browned.

2. Add the garlic, cook for a further minute, then tip in the beef and stir well. Cook for 6–8 minutes until the beef is cooked and any liquid excess has evaporated.

3. Add the Worcestershire and Tabasco sauces and cook for a further minute. Add the tomato purée and ketchup, stir well and cook for another minute.

4. Add the roasted red peppers and mix well. Cook for 5–10 minutes. Season with a little salt and pepper; you should only need a small amount of salt.

5. Meanwhile, toast the cut sides of the buns.

6. Divide the mixture among the toasted burger buns, sandwich together and serve immediately.

FRIED CHICKEN SANDWICH

SERVES 4

INGREDIENTS

VEGETABLE OIL, FOR DEEP FRYING

4 BUNS, HALVED

12 SLICES OF GHERKIN

¼ ICEBERG LETTUCE, FINELY SHREDDED

100g MAYONNAISE

For the marinade

300ml BUTTERMILK

1 TSP FINE SEA SALT

½ TSP ONION POWDER

¼ TSP GARLIC POWDER

¼ TSP SWEET SMOKED PAPRIKA

4 SMALL CHICKEN BREASTS

For the spiced flour

½ TSP ONION POWDER

¼ TSP GARLIC POWDER

½ TSP SWEET SMOKED PAPRIKA

½ TSP GROUND WHITE PEPPER

½ TSP GROUND BLACK PEPPER

½ TSP MUSTARD POWDER

1½ TSP FINE SEA SALT

100g PLAIN FLOUR

25g WHITE RICE FLOUR

METHOD

1. For the marinade, beat the buttermilk, salt, onion and garlic powder, and paprika in a mixing bowl with a fork or balloon whisk. Make sure there are no lumps. Add the chicken and stir to coat. Cover and leave to marinate in the fridge for up to 48 hours (see Introduction on page 120).

2. For the spiced flour, whisk all the ingredients well in a large mixing bowl.

3. When ready to cook the chicken, heat a deep-fat fryer to 160°C (325°F), or pour enough oil into a large, deep saucepan to come one-third of the way up the sides. Heat the oil over a medium heat until it reaches 160°C (325°F). A cooking thermometer is useful but not essential. (A cube of white bread will brown in 60 seconds if the oil is at the right temperature.)

4. While the oil is heating, remove the chicken pieces from the marinade, shaking off all but a little of the excess buttermilk. Toss in the spiced flour, making sure each piece of chicken is covered.

5. Cook the chicken pieces in the hot oil, in batches, for 12 minutes until golden and cooked through. Every time you add new pieces of chicken, the temperature of the oil will drop. Try to maintain the temperature between 150°C (300°F) and 160°C (325°F) throughout the cooking process by adjusting the temperature of the heat below the oil.

6. Meanwhile, toast the cut sides of the buns.

7. Place the shredded lettuce on the bottom halves of the buns and top with 3 slices of gherkin.

8. Spread a spoonful of mayonnaise on both halves of the buns.

9. Remove each piece of chicken carefully with a slotted spoon or "spider", drain briefly on kitchen paper and place on top of the lettuce.

10. Bring the 2 halves of the buns together and serve.

TRIPLE GRILLED CHEESE

SERVES 4

The ultimate midnight snack.
Strictly speaking, this is quadruple grilled cheese: Fred has switched the usual butter for mascarpone
for the extra creaminess. This would work well with Pickled Red Onions (see page 90) inside
and a bowl of Byron Sauce for dipping (see page 88).

INGREDIENTS

4 TBSP MASCARPONE

8 SLICES OF BRIOCHE BREAD

100g GRATED CHEDDAR CHEESE

140g GRATED COMTÉ CHEESE,
(OR GRUYÈRE OR EMMENTHAL)

UNSALTED BUTTER, SOFTENED, FOR GREASING

50g FINELY GRATED PARMESAN CHEESE

METHOD

1. Spread the mascarpone over one side of the slices of bread.

2. Mix all the Cheddar and two-thirds of the Comté. Scatter this over 4 of the slices of bread. Sandwich together with the remaining slices, making sure the mascarpone is on the inside.

3. Place a large frying pan over a medium heat. Spread some butter over the outside of the bread. Scatter half the grated Parmesan over the buttered side of the sandwiches, then top with half the remaining Comté. Push the cheeses gently into the buttered bread. Turn the sandwiches over and repeat on the other side using more butter, and the remaining Parmesan and Comté.

4. Place the sandwiches in the hot pan, in batches if necessary, and cook until dark gold on the underside. Press the sandwiches down gently now and again with the back of a fish slice or with a spatula.

5. Turn the sandwiches over carefully and continue to cook, pressing down gently now and again with the fish slice or spatula and reducing the heat to low, until the cheese begins to run and the outsides are golden.

6. To serve, cut the sandwiches in half and serve while the cheese is still oozing.

TALL TALE № 06 — THE LAST COACH OUT OF NAPA VALLEY

When you're in San Francisco, one of the absolute must-dos is a trip to Napa Valley to visit the vineyards that produce some of the finest wines in the world. And when we headed to California for our "Big Trip", we did just that. Our reputation must have preceded us, because when we arrived, our hosts informed us that we were skipping the usual walking tour and cracking straight on with the important part - the tasting. We weren't going to argue with that.

Many, many bottles, vertical tastings and vintages down, it was time to leave. The first coach - and the first merry departees - rolled back down the road to San Fran, but the second coach had a puncture, and there was nothing for

it but to fill the hours with more - ahem - tastings. By the time the coach was finally roadworthy again, and we were on our way (two extra cases of wine in tow, gifted by our hosts), its passengers were doing a pretty good job of impersonating the last days of Rome. There were stumblings and fumblings in the aisle. There were definitely some very unwell people. There were flaring tempers. There were ill-advised passionate embraces. And to top things off, the air conditioning broke. I'll say no more...

I often shudder to think what that coach driver made of us. If he's reading this, and he ever comes to the UK - the drinks are definitely on me.

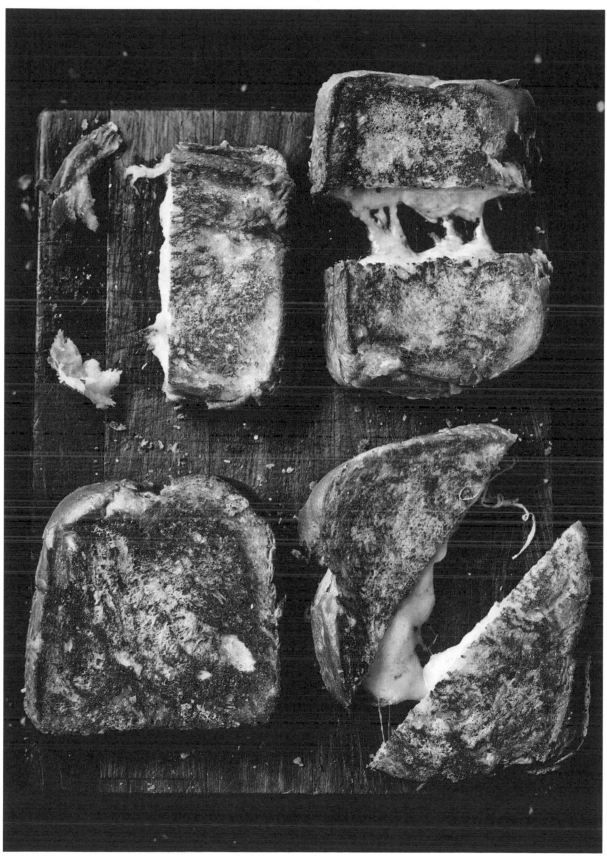

CLUB SANDWICH

SERVES 4

We love club sandwiches but, too often, they arrive unpalatably dry.
This recipe avoids that by using egg mayonnaise instead of hard-boiled eggs.

INGREDIENTS

12 SLICES OF GOOD-QUALITY WHITE BREAD

3 CHAR-GRILLED MARINATED CHICKEN BREASTS
(SEE PAGE 143), SLICED

BYRON SAUCE (SEE PAGE 88)

2 BABY GEM LETTUCES, OUTER LEAVES
DISCARDED, LEAVES SEPARATED

12 SLICES OF CRISPY SMOKED STREAKY BACON
(SEE PAGE 94)

2 TOMATOES, THINLY SLICED

For the egg mayonnaise

4 FRIDGE-COLD MEDIUM EGGS

4 TBSP FINELY CHOPPED CHIVES

150g MAYONNAISE

SEA SALT AND FRESHLY GROUND BLACK PEPPER

METHOD

1. For the egg mayonnaise, bring a saucepan of water to the boil and then gently add the eggs. Simmer for 8 minutes exactly, then transfer the eggs to a bowl of iced water to cool quickly.

2. Shell and dice the eggs. Add them to a bowl with the chives, mayonnaise, a pinch of salt and a few good grinds of black pepper. Mix gently until combined. Taste and adjust the seasoning, then set aside.

3. Lightly toast the slices of bread.

4. On one slice of bread, place a layer of egg mayonnaise and top with slices of the Char-grilled Marinated Chicken Breast.

5. On another slice of bread, place a spoonful of Byron Sauce, a few lettuce leaves and 3 slices of Crispy Smoked Streaky Bacon.

6. On the final slice of bread, add a spoonful of Byron Sauce and 3 slices of tomato.

7. Bring the 3 slices together and serve.

MEATBALL SANDWICHES

SERVES 4

INGREDIENTS

1 QUANTITY OF MEATBALLS (SEE PAGE 116)

4 SUB ROLLS, HALVED

2 BALLS OF MOZZARELLA, DRAINED SLICED INTO 6

OLIVE OIL, TO DRIZZLE

METHOD

1. Preheat the grill to high.

2. In a medium–large saucepan, reheat the Meatballs in their tomato sauce, until warmed through.

3. Lightly toast or grill the cut sides of the sub rolls.

4. Meanwhile, place a slice of mozzarella over each meatball in the pan and cover with a lid. Cook over a medium heat for 2–3 minutes or until the cheese has melted.

5. Drizzle the insides of the rolls with a little olive oil. Spread a little tomato sauce onto the bottom of the rolls.

6. Place 3 meatballs over the tomato sauce, pushing them down onto the roll to help them balance. Spread the remaining tomato sauce over the top halves of the rolls and add the top of the roll.

CHAPTER 6

SALADS

You might be surprised to learn that salads are a big part of the American diner experience. Typically, the restaurants throw in other ingredients such as bacon, cheese and creamy dressings that tend to mitigate some of the health benefits.

AN ICEBERG WEDGE IS THE PERFECT ACCOMPANIMENT TO A BURGER: BRIGHT AND REFRESHING BUT WITH THE RICH CREAMINESS OF BLUE CHEESE.

It's the best way to showcase an unfairly maligned lettuce variety. We often use escarole in the restaurants because of the way its rippled leaves catch the juices in a burger – but iceberg has an unassailable crunch.

Some of the recipes in this chapter, such as the Cobb and avocado ranch salads, are part of the classic American diner experience. Others, including the Niçoise and Greek salads, are here because they work beautifully at barbecues and other summer events. Fred and I have kept the methods traditional, on the whole, with no weird twists or zany additions. They became classics for good reason, and we'd be the last people to tinker with that

CLASSIC CAESAR SALAD

SERVES 4

Whenever Fred is invited to a barbecue, his friends always ask him to bring along his Caesar salad.
The key is to use the best ingredients you can find: top-quality anchovies, good oil and fresh free-range eggs.
To make this a heartier salad, slice two Char-grilled Marinated Chicken Breasts (see page 143) and add to the plates
at the end, at the same time as the anchovies.

INGREDIENTS

2 LARGE COS, 3 ROMAINE, OR 10 BABY GEM
LETTUCES, OUTER LEAVES DISCARDED,
LEAVES SEPARATED AND SLICED

1 QUANTITY OF CROÛTONS (SEE PAGE 142)

75G PARMESAN CHEESE SHAVINGS

8 ANCHOVIES IN OLIVE OIL, DRAINED

For the dressing

2 ANCHOVIES IN OLIVE OIL, DRAINED AND
VERY FINELY CHOPPED

1 GARLIC CLOVE, FINELY CRUSHED

1 MEDIUM EGG YOLK

3 TBSP FINELY GRATED PARMESAN CHEESE

JUICE OF ¼ LEMON

½ TSP RED WINE VINEGAR

75ML OLIVE OIL

75ML VEGETABLE OR SUNFLOWER OIL

SEA SALT AND FRESHLY GROUND BLACK PEPPER

METHOD

1. For the dressing, put the anchovies, garlic, egg yolk, Parmesan, lemon juice and vinegar in a large mixing bowl. Beat with a balloon whisk to combine. Mix the oils in a small jug. Whisking continuously, slowly pour the oils into the bowl, making sure to whisk as you pour so the dressing doesn't separate. If you are alone in the kitchen, with no one to help hold your mixing bowl, you might find it helpful to put a slightly wet cloth or kitchen paper under the bowl to stop it from moving around.

2. When all the oil has been added and the dressing is emulsified, taste and season with salt and pepper as needed. If the dressing is slightly thicker than you normally like, whisk in 1 tablespoon cold water.

3. To serve, add the lettuce and Croûtons to the dressing. Toss well.

4. Divide the salad among 4 plates and scatter the shaved Parmesan over the top. Garnish each salad with 2 anchovies and serve.

GREEK SALAD

SERVES 4

Fred used to make this during a stint working at a London restaurant called Ransome's Dock.
His sister is obsessed with this dish.

INGREDIENTS

500g CHERRY TOMATOES, HALVED

180g PITTED KALAMATA OLIVES

1 SMALL RED ONION, VERY THINLY SLICED

500g CUCUMBER, TRIMMED AND CUBED

2 TBSP DRIED OREGANO

400g DRAINED AND CUBED GOOD-QUALITY FETA CHEESE

For the dressing

JUICE OF 1 LEMON

150ml EXTRA VIRGIN OLIVE OIL

SEA SALT AND FRESHLY GROUND BLACK PEPPER

METHOD

1. Put all the ingredients for the salad in a large mixing bowl and gently toss.

2. For the dressing, whisk together the lemon juice and olive oil in a small bowl until combined. Taste and season with salt and pepper.

3. Pour the dressing over the salad and mix thoroughly but gently. Serve the salad, either in a large salad bowl/platter or on individual plates.

POKER FACE

TALL TALE
Nº 07

Racer 5 IPA is legendary among American craft-beer connoisseurs – and its creator, Richard C. Norgrove II, the eccentric founder of Bear Republic Brewing Co., is a greater legend still. I had set my heart on securing some of his strictly limited Racer 5 for Byron's budding craft-beer list, even if it meant begging Mr Norgrove myself. And so it was that I found myself driving for hours north of San Francisco to do just that.

When I finally reached Bear Republic HQ, I was met with blank looks. Mr Norgrove certainly wasn't there, and nobody had any record of an appointment between him and a hot and travel-weary Englishman. In fact, they'd never heard of me. It took all the charm I could still muster to discover that I might just find him

at his brewpub – an hour back in the direction I had come.

The brewpub that afternoon was dimly lit and quiet, the only sound the careful slap of cards on the table in the corner as a poker game progressed. The barmaid told me, reverentially, that one of the players was Richard Norgrove himself. I introduced myself as best I could.

"All the way from London, you say? Really? Fine. Let's talk. But only after I've won this game." I sat down to wait.

A mere hour or two later, he'd won the game – and I'd won myself a couple of pallets of Racer 5 for the restaurants.

COBB SALAD

SERVES 4

Bob Cobb, a 1920s Los Angeles restaurateur, allegedly invented this dish as a way to use up leftovers, but we think it's worth doing for its own sake. In the restaurants, we line up the ingredients neatly on the plates. If you prefer to scatter everything more haphazardly, it will taste just as good.

INGREDIENTS

½ ICEBERG LETTUCE, SLICED

4 HANDFULS OF BABY SPINACH LEAVES
(APPROX. 150G)

8 SLICES OF CRISPY SMOKED STREAKY
BACON (SEE PAGE 94), DICED

100G BLUE CHEESE, CUT INTO 1CM CUBES

4 MEDIUM TOMATOES, CUT INTO 1CM CUBES

2 CHAR-GRILLED MARINATED CHICKEN BREASTS
(SEE PAGE 143), CUT INTO 1CM CUBES

4 HARD-BOILED EGGS, PEELED AND CUT
INTO 1CM CUBES

2 RIPE AVOCADOS, CUT INTO 1CM CUBES

4 TBSP FINELY CHOPPED CHIVES

For the dressing

1 TBSP DIJON MUSTARD

2 TBSP WHITE WINE VINEGAR

125ML EXTRA VIRGIN OLIVE OIL

SEA SALT AND FRESHLY GROUND BLACK PEPPER

METHOD

1. Place the lettuce and spinach on
4 serving plates.

2. Line up all the rest of the salad
ingredients over the lettuce and
spinach.

3. For the dressing, whisk together the
mustard and vinegar in a small bowl.
Slowly pour in the olive oil, whisking
continuously. The dressing should be
thick and creamy looking. Taste and
season with salt and pepper.

4. Sprinkle over the chopped chives
and serve with the dressing on the side
or poured over the salad.

SALAD NIÇOISE

SERVES 4

There appears to be a wholly inappropriate modern tendency to use fresh tuna in this dish.
The classic recipe demands good-quality tinned fish, which we prefer. You want the eggs to be just set.

INGREDIENTS

6 PLUM TOMATOES

1 BUNCH OF BASIL, LEAVES ONLY,
FINELY SHREDDED

100ML EXTRA VIRGIN OLIVE OIL

12 NEW POTATOES (ABOUT 350G)

200G GREEN BEANS, TOPPED, TAILED
AND HALVED

4 FRIDGE-COLD MEDIUM EGGS

2 COS OR ROMAINE LETTUCES,
OUTER LEAVES DISCARDED

125G PITTED BLACK OLIVES, E.G. KALAMATA

1 TIN OF ANCHOVIES IN OLIVE OIL, DRAINED

400G DRAINED GOOD-QUALITY TINNED TUNA
IN OLIVE OIL

SEA SALT AND FRESHLY GROUND BLACK PEPPER

For the dressing

1 TBSP DIJON MUSTARD

2 TBSP WHITE WINE VINEGAR

125ML EXTRA VIRGIN OLIVE OIL

METHOD

1. Quarter the tomatoes and place in a medium mixing bowl. Add the basil leaves, olive oil and a couple of decent pinches of salt. Toss until evenly coated, then set aside.

2. Bring a medium saucepan of water to the boil, add a generous pinch of salt and simmer the potatoes until tender. Drain and refresh the potatoes in a bowl of iced water. Drain again and pat dry with kitchen paper.

3. Bring a small saucepan of water to the boil, add a pinch of salt and simmer the beans for 3 minutes. Drain and refresh the beans in the same way you did the potatoes, then drain again and pat dry.

4. Bring a saucepan of water to the boil and then gently add the eggs. Simmer for 8 minutes and refresh in iced water. Shell and quarter the eggs, being careful not to lose any yolk.

5. For the dressing, whisk the mustard and vinegar together in a small bowl. Slowly pour in the olive oil, whisking continuously. The dressing should be thick and creamy. Taste and season with salt and pepper.

6. To assemble the salad, take 4 serving plates or a large platter. Slice the lettuces, discarding the stalks, and divide the leaves among the plates.

7. Halve the potatoes and place on top of the lettuce. Add the marinated tomatoes, draining off any excess oil, and then the eggs.

8. Scatter the olives, green beans and anchovies evenly over the plates.

9. Top with the tuna, putting it in the middle of the plates, and season it with a grinding of black pepper.

10. Serve with the dressing in little pots on the side or poured over the salad.

AVOCADO RANCH SALAD

SERVES 4

A good, substantial, earthy salad, and an appropriate showcase for ranch dressing.

INGREDIENTS

200g GREEN BEANS, TOPPED, TAILED AND HALVED

½ LONG CUCUMBER

1 COS LETTUCE, SLICED

70g ROCKET

300g CHERRY TOMATOES, HALVED

200g RADISHES, TOPPED, TAILED AND SLICED

2 ROASTED RED PEPPERS – SHOP-BOUGHT AND DRAINED, OR SEE RECIPE ON PAGE 95 – SLICED

1 QUANTITY OF CROÛTONS (SEE PAGE 142)

2 RIPE AVOCADOS

RANCH DRESSING (SEE PAGE 82)

A COUPLE OF PINCHES OF SWEET SMOKED PAPRIKA

SEA SALT

METHOD

1. Bring a small saucepan of water to the boil, add a pinch of salt and boil the beans for 3 minutes. Drain and refresh in iced water, then drain again and pat dry with kitchen paper.

2. Slice the cucumber on the diagonal into slices about 5mm wide. Cut each of these slices into 3.

3. Arrange the lettuce and rocket on 4 plates. Scatter the green beans, cucumber slices, tomatoes, radishes, roasted red peppers and homemade Croûtons over the top, making sure that everything is evenly distributed.

4. Halve the avocados and remove their stones. Peel the avocado halves, trying to keep the flesh intact. Slice the avocado halves and spread them over the salad.

5. Drizzle the Ranch Dressing on the salad and sprinkle over the sweet smoked paprika.

THE CLASSIC AMERICAN-DINER
ICEBERG WEDGE

SERVES 4

This dish represents much of what we try to do at Byron: to re-introduce people to the classics of the American diner. There is simply no better way to eat an iceberg lettuce.

INGREDIENTS

1 ICEBERG LETTUCE WITH TIGHTLY PACKED LEAVES

BLUE CHEESE DRESSING (SEE PAGE 85), CHILLED

1 QUANTITY OF CROÛTONS (SEE PAGE 142)

8 SLICES OF CRISPY SMOKED STREAKY BACON (SEE PAGE 94), DICED

2 TBSP FINELY CHOPPED CHIVES

METHOD

1. Slice the lettuce through the core into 4 wedges. Discard any wilted outer leaves and trim off most of the stalk while keeping the wedge intact. Place each wedge, on its back, on 4 serving plates.

2. Stir the Blue Cheese Dressing, then spoon it over the wedges, almost entirely covering each piece.

3. Scatter the homemade Croûtons around the wedges and sprinkle over the diced Crispy Smoked Streaky Bacon. Throw on the chives and serve.

"ARE YOU EVER GOING TO FINISH THAT RESTAURANT?"

We took over our Islington restaurant in north London from (shhh) another hamburger joint, who'd sold the site to us. By the time we'd stripped the place back to its bones, we weren't really in the mood to smarten it up again. We'd already given our first Soho restaurant a New York-industrial design, inspired by some of my favourite places in downtown Manhattan — so our designer Clare thought it might be fun to see just how far we could push that look in the middle of chichi Islington.

Come by the restaurant today and you'll find bare beams, lightbulbs swinging from their wires, half-finished coatings of plaster and unsanded floorboards that reveal layer after layer of paint.

Even though it is now a much replicated look, not a week goes by without someone getting in touch to ask us whether we're ever planning on finishing that building site of a restaurant. Whether it's an attempt at wit or a genuine complaint we're never quite sure, but as long as the restaurant stays full of happy customers, we'll leave it as it is.

CROÛTONS

MAKES ENOUGH FOR 4 SALADS

If you happen to have some bread that needs eating at home, then by all means use that instead of the baguette.
It's a brilliant way to use up bread that is past its best.
At the restaurants we use the burger buns that are no longer squidgy enough.

INGREDIENTS

½ LONG BAGUETTE (APPROX. 150g IN TOTAL)

2 TBSP OLIVE OIL

SEA SALT AND FRESHLY GROUND BLACK PEPPER

METHOD

1. Preheat the oven to 160°C (325°F).

2. With the crust still on, cut the baguette into 2cm cubes. Put these in a large mixing bowl and drizzle with the olive oil. Add ½ teaspoon salt and a couple of grinds of pepper. Mix well so that each cube is seasoned and oiled. Use your hands if you like. Tip the cubes onto a large baking tray.

3. Bake in the preheated oven for 15 minutes until the bread is lightly browned, giving the cubes a stir every now and again.

4. Remove the baking tray from the oven and leave the croûtons to cool completely before storing in an airtight container. They should stay crunchy for up to 5 days.

CHAR-GRILLED MARINATED CHICKEN BREASTS

MAKES ENOUGH FOR 4 BURGERS, BUT HALVE THE RECIPE FOR MOST SALADS

INGREDIENTS

4 CHICKEN BREASTS

3 TBSP BUTTERMILK

3 TBSP OLIVE, SUNFLOWER OR VEGETABLE OIL, PLUS A LITTLE EXTRA FOR COOKING

1¼ TSP ONION POWDER

A HANDFUL OF PARSLEY LEAVES

FRESHLY GROUND BLACK PEPPER

METHOD

1. First butterfly the chicken breasts: place one breast on a chopping board with the thickest part facing away from you. Slice the chicken breast almost in half horizontally, stopping about 1cm before the other side. You will be left with a piece of chicken you can open out like a book, but that is still attached along the middle. Alternatively, your butcher to do this. If the chicken breasts still have their mini fillets attached, you can cut these away and add them to the marinade. They are perfect for the salads.

2. To make the marinade, blend the buttermilk, oil, onion powder, parsley leaves and a couple of grinds of pepper in a food processor or with a stick blender.

3. Put the chicken breasts in a freezer bag or similar and pour the marinade over them, mixing really well to ensure every bit of chicken is covered, including the insides of the breasts where they have been cut. Cover well and refrigerate for up to 3 days.

4. To cook the chicken, heat a dash of oil in a large, heavy-bottomed ridged pan over a medium high heat. Add the chicken breasts, opened out so they are as flat as possible. Cook for 4 minutes, reducing the heat slightly if the chicken is browning too quickly. You want some charred, dark bits on the breasts, but not for them to be burnt.

5. Flip the chicken over and cook for another 4 minutes or until cooked through. Remove the pan from the heat and leave the chicken to rest for 2–3 minutes. Enjoy immediately, for example in the Chicken Burger (see page 52) or leave to cool for use in salads.

CHAPTER 7

Desserts

This book is about good American food – and that, of course, includes good American desserts. No fruit salads or sorbets here: just unashamedly indulgent dishes that echo the sweeter, simpler tastes of childhood. I've always thought that the key difference between British and American desserts is that we tend to use more fruit for sweetness, while the best American sweets are unafraid of sugar. Regardless, there are some absolute showstoppers here.

My favourite is the Byron cheesecake. Set rather than baked, with a perfect texture and creaminess, it's surprisingly easy to make. You may never need another brownie recipe after you've tasted ours: it's as dense and fudgy as anyone could hope for. There is something inherently hospitable about flour and sugar, combined and cooked with attention and love.

And what could be finer than a plate of chocolate chip cookies with a glass of cold milk?

Nothing is particularly fancy in this chapter, and we've made sure that the methods stay faithful to their largely humble origins. You'll find these recipes ideal for birthdays and dinner parties, as well as solitary treats.

Chocolate Brownies

MAKES 12–16, DEPENDING ON SIZE

Everyone has a view on the perfect brownie.
Ours are unapologetically gooey rather than hard in the middle: the magic lies in the contrast with the crispy crust.
The cooking time is critical: follow the recipe closely for guaranteed success.

INGREDIENTS

210g GOOD-QUALITY DARK CHOCOLATE (70% COCOA SOLIDS), BROKEN INTO PIECES

225g UNSALTED BUTTER, CUBED

1½ TSP INSTANT COFFEE GRANULES

3 MEDIUM EGGS

300g CASTER SUGAR

¼ TSP FINE SEA SALT

100g PLAIN FLOUR

METHOD

1. Preheat the oven to 160°C (325°F). Line a 20–23cm square baking tin with parchment paper.

2. Put the chocolate, butter and coffee granules in a medium heatproof bowl. Bring a small saucepan, a quarter-full of water, to a gentle simmer. Place the bowl on top, resting on the edge of the pan, so that no part of it touches the water. Turn down the heat to a gentle simmer and leave until the butter and chocolate have completely melted, stirring now and again. Remove the bowl from the pan and leave to cool slightly.

3. Meanwhile, put the eggs, sugar and salt in a mixing bowl and beat with an electric whisk (or by hand with a balloon whisk) until thick, pale, creamy and almost doubled in size. This could take up to 5 minutes, or considerably longer by hand.

4. Beat in the chocolate mixture until completely combined. Tip in the flour and beat again, stopping when all the flour is mixed in. Once the flour is added, do not beat for more than 1 minute or you risk over-mixing and making the brownies tough.

5. Tip the mixture into the baking tin and bake for 40 minutes, or until just set. After 35 minutes, give the tin a little shake: if the middle still wobbles then it needs another 5 minutes. A skewer inserted into the middle of the brownie should come out with crumbs, but not a huge amount of raw mixture. This will give a gooey, but set brownie. Remove the tin from the oven and leave the brownies to cool in the tin.

6. Remove the brownies from the tin, cut into portions and serve. Any leftover brownies can be stored in an airtight container for up to 5 days.

Byron Cheesecake with Blueberries

SERVES 10-12

*An easy pudding with a base that is set in the fridge rather than baked.
It's very popular with our teams in the restaurants. You can make it in a 23cm round springform cake tin,
or a 20cm one which will give in a deeper crust and taller cheesecake.
Note that the cheesecake needs to set overnight (or for at least 10 hours).*

INGREDIENTS

For the base

250g DIGESTIVE BISCUITS

125g UNSALTED BUTTER, MELTED

For the filling

400g WHITE CHOCOLATE, CHOPPED

100ml DOUBLE CREAM

850g FULL-FAT CREAM CHEESE

150g CASTER SUGAR

JUICE OF 2 LIMES

1 TSP VANILLA EXTRACT

For the blueberry topping

120g HONEY

JUICE OF 1 LEMON

500g FRESH OR FROZEN BLUEBERRIES

METHOD

1. Line the base and sides of a 20–23cm round springform cake tin with parchment paper.

2. Blitz the biscuits in a food processor until they resemble breadcrumbs.

3. Pour the melted butter into the food processor and blend well.

4. Tip the crumb mixture into the cake tin and flatten with the back of a spoon to form an even layer. Place in the fridge to firm up while you make the filling.

5. For the filling, put the chocolate and cream in a medium heatproof bowl. Bring a small saucepan, a quarter-full of water, to a gentle simmer. Place the heatproof bowl on top, resting on the edge of the pan, so that no part of the bowl touches the water. Turn down the heat to a gentle simmer and leave until the chocolate has just melted, stirring now and again to mix. With white chocolate, you may find the mixture looks like it's separating slightly but simply give it a good stir and it will come back together.

6. Clean the bowl of the food processor and dry it well. Put the remaining filling ingredients in the processor and blitz. Now spoon in the melted chocolate mixture and mix well.

7. Remove the cake tin from the fridge and spoon the filling into the tin over the base. Cover and return the cake tin to the fridge. Leave to set for at least 10 hours; it can be made up to 24 hours in advance.

8. To make the blueberry topping, put the honey and lemon juice in a medium saucepan and bring to a simmer. Tip in the blueberries and stir to coat them in the lemon and honey. Bring back to a simmer and, as soon as the blueberries begin to bubble, remove the pan from the heat. Leave to cool, then transfer to a bowl, cover and refrigerate until ready to use.

9. When ready to serve, carefully remove the cheesecake from the tin. Fill a bowl with hot water and dip a sharp knife to warm it. Dry the knife and slice the cheesecake into wedges.

10. Serve with the blueberries and some of their syrup.

Banoffee Pie

SERVES 8

A British classic, and a terrific do-ahead pudding that pleases everyone.

INGREDIENTS

For the base

200g DIGESTIVE BISCUITS

110g UNSALTED BUTTER, MELTED

1 TSP VANILLA EXTRACT

For the topping

400g DULCE DE LECHE OR CARNATION CARAMEL

3-4 BANANAS, PEELED AND SLICED

400ml DOUBLE CREAM

25g CASTER SUGAR

COCOA POWDER, TO SERVE

METHOD

1. Line the base and sides of a 20cm round springform cake tin with parchment paper.

2. Blitz the biscuits in a food processor until they resemble breadcrumbs. Pour the melted butter and vanilla into the food processor and blend well.

3. Tip the crumb mixture into the prepared cake tin and flatten with the back of a spoon. Place in the fridge to firm up for 20 minutes.

4. Once the base is firm, spoon the dulce de leche over the biscuit base and spread it level.

5. Arrange the sliced bananas evenly over the top and press them down gently into the dulce de leche.

6. Whip the cream and sugar in a mixing bowl until stiff peaks form. Spoon over the pie and spread out evenly. Return to the fridge for up to 1 hour.

7. When ready to serve, carefully remove the banoffee pie from the tin. Dust a little cocoa powder over the top of the pie and cut into slices.

WOULD YOU LIKE SOME BOURBON WITH THAT BOURBON?

I'd always thought that bourbon deserved a better rep, and once we'd decided to introduce it to the menu, there could only be one next move. A research trip was on the cards. A tough gig, sure, but luckily my intrepid right-hand man Peter was good enough to volunteer himself.

Armed with advice and letters of introduction from my friend Jamie Berger of Pitt Cue Co., who knows more than most about American whiskey, we landed in Louisville, Kentucky – the epicentre of the bourbon world.

Our distinguished guide was Bill Samuels III, president of Makers Mark, who took us around all the best distilleries, bars and restaurants. We soon discovered that in Kentucky, they put bourbon in everything. Bourbon in barbecue sauce, bourbon in gravy (to go with your biscuits), bourbon hard sauce on ice cream. Even bourbon in your coffee. Nothing is safe. There is just no escaping the stuff.

As a finale, we found ourselves – fittingly enough – in a bar called Meat. Their off-menu speciality is a drink called Coke Dick Motorcycle. It's a refreshing blend of moonshine, green Chartreuse, and (obviously) bourbon. And, after a long day's tasting, that drink was what finally did it for Peter.

Funnily enough, while we ended up with a bourbon list to be proud of, the Coke Dick Motorcycle never made it onto the Byron menu.

Oreo Cheesecake

SERVES 10–12

You will need about four packets of Oreo cookies for this,
and be warned that the cheesecake is best left to set overnight.

INGREDIENTS

For the base

22 OREO COOKIES

100g UNSALTED BUTTER, MELTED

For the filling

700g FULL-FAT CREAM CHEESE

1 TBSP VANILLA EXTRACT

150g CASTER SUGAR

JUICE OF 1 LIME

200ml DOUBLE CREAM

20 OREO COOKIES, ROUGHLY CHOPPED

For the topping

10 OREO COOKIES

METHOD

1. Line the base and sides of a 20cm round springform cake tin with parchment paper.

2. For the base, blitz the Oreo cookies in a food processor until crumb-like.

3. Pour the melted butter into the food processor and blend.

4. Tip the crumb mixture into the prepared cake tin and flatten with the back of a spoon. Place in the fridge to firm up.

5. For the filling, clean the bowl of the food processor and dry well. Put all the filling ingredients except the Oreos in the food processor and blitz for 1 minute. The mixture should be shiny and smooth. Now add the chopped Oreo cookies and blitz for a few seconds to combine.

6. Remove the tin from the fridge and spoon in filling. Cover and return to the fridge. Leave the cheesecake to set for at least 10 hours; it can be made up to 24 hours in advance.

7. For the topping, blitz the Oreo cookies until crumb-like. Scatter evenly over the top of the cheesecake. You can do this straight after making the filling or the following day, just before serving.

8. When ready to serve, carefully remove the cheesecake from the tin. Fill a bowl with hot water and dip a sharp knife to warm it. Dry the knife and slice the cheesecake into wedges.

9. Serve the cheesecake proudly on its own.

Cherry Pie

SERVES 6–8

Fred partly grew up in America. His mum, who has a sweet tooth,
would always order cherry pie during their frequent trips to the diner.
Here is a recipe to make any mum with a sweet tooth smile.

INGREDIENTS

1.2kg PITTED FRESH, FROZEN OR CANNED AND DRAINED SWEET CHERRIES

100-150g CASTER SUGAR, PLUS AN EXTRA TBSP FOR THE TOP

30g CORNFLOUR

JUICE OF ½ LEMON

10g UNSALTED BUTTER

1 MEDIUM EGG WHITE, LIGHTLY BEATEN

For the pastry

400g PLAIN FLOUR

25g CASTER SUGAR

A PINCH OF FINE SEA SALT

250g VERY COLD, UNSALTED BUTTER, CUBED

METHOD

1. Grease a 23–25cm pie dish with butter.

2. Preheat the oven to 180°C (350°F).

3. For the pastry, put the flour, caster sugar and salt into the bowl of a food processor. Blitz briefly, then add the butter and blitz until the mixture resembles breadcrumbs.

4. Add 5 tablespoons very cold water and blitz until the mixture comes together into a ball.

5. Remove the dough from the food processor and divide into 2. Flatten these into discs about 2cm thick, wrap well in clingfilm and refrigerate for 15–20 minutes to firm up. If it's still too soft to work with, put it back in the fridge or freezer until firm.

6. Meanwhile, put the pitted cherries, 100g of the sugar, the cornflour and lemon juice in a mixing bowl. Mix and then set aside while the pastry firms up.

7. When the pastry is firm, take one of the pastry discs out of the fridge and place between 2 sheets of parchment paper on the work surface. Using a rolling pin, roll the pastry until 5mm thick and wide enough to cover the base of your pie dish with a little overlapping the sides.

8. Line the pie dish with the pastry sheet, making sure it is centred and you have some pastry hanging over the edge. Gently push the pastry into the edges of the pie dish, being careful not to tear it.

9. Stir the cherry mixture again. Taste it and add a little more sugar if necessary. Pour the cherries into the pie dish and dot the butter over them.

10. Roll out the remaining pastry disc as before. Brush the edge of the pastry in the pie dish with egg white, then top the pie with the second pastry sheet. Trim the edges with a sharp knife.

11. Crimp the sheets of pastry together along the edge of the dish to seal the pie, then cut a couple of small slits in the pastry lid to allow steam to escape during baking.

12. Brush the pastry lid with the remaining egg white and sprinkle over the extra tablespoon of sugar. Place the dish on a roasting tray and bake for 45–50 minutes or until the pastry is a dark golden brown and the filling is bubbling.

13. Remove the pie from the oven and leave to cool slightly before serving. Once cold, you can store the pie wrapped in clingfilm for up to 24 hours, but not in the fridge.

Apple Pie

SERVES 6-8

A quintessentially American sweet. Apple chunks within the purée provide a more interesting texture.

INGREDIENTS

5 LARGE BRAMLEY APPLES (APPROX. 1.5KG IN TOTAL), PEELED, CORED AND CUT INTO CHUNKS

¾ TSP GROUND CINNAMON

¼ TSP FRESHLY GRATED NUTMEG

JUICE OF ½ LEMON

200–250G DEMERARA SUGAR, PLUS 1 EXTRA TBSP FOR THE TOP

5 BRAEBURN, COX OR OTHER EATING APPLES (APPROX. 800G), PEELED, CORED AND CUT INTO CHUNKS

1 MEDIUM EGG WHITE, LIGHTLY BEATEN

WHIPPED CREAM, TO SERVE

For the pastry

400G PLAIN FLOUR

25G CASTER SUGAR

A PINCH OF FINE SEA SALT

250G VERY COLD, UNSALTED BUTTER, CUBED

METHOD

1. Grease a 23–25cm pie dish with butter.

2. Preheat the oven to 180°C (350°F).

3. For the pastry, put the flour, caster sugar and salt into the bowl of a food processor. Blitz briefly, add the butter and blitz until the mixture resembles breadcrumbs.

4. Add 5 tablespoons very cold water and blitz until the mixture comes together into a ball.

5. Remove the dough from the food processor and divide into 2. Flatten these into discs about 2cm thick, wrap well in clingfilm and refrigerate for 15–20 minutes to firm up. If it's still too soft to work with, put it back in the fridge or freezer until firm.

6. Meanwhile, put the chunks of Bramley apple, spices, lemon juice and 200g of the demerara sugar into a medium-large saucepan over a medium heat. Stir for a few minutes and when hot, reduce the heat to medium-low. Cook for 20–25 minutes, stirring often, until the apples have broken down into a fluffy purée. Remove from the heat and leave to cool until just warm.

7. When the apple purée has cooled, take one of the pastry discs out of the fridge and place between 2 sheets of parchment paper on the work surface. Using a rolling pin, roll the pastry until 5mm thick and wide enough to cover the base of your pie dish with a little pastry overlapping the sides.

8. Line the pie dish with the pastry sheet, making sure it is centred and you have some pastry hanging over the edge. Gently push the pastry into the edges of the pie dish, being careful not to tear it.

9. Mix the whole chunks of eating apple into the cooled apple purée. Taste the mixture and add a little more sugar if necessary. Spread the mixture in the pie dish, creating a slight dome in the middle.

10. Roll out the remaining pastry disc in the same way as before. Brush the edge of the pastry in the pie dish with egg white, then top the pie with the second pastry sheet. Trim the edges with a sharp knife.

11. Crimp the sheets of pastry together along the edge of the dish to seal the pie, then cut a couple of small slits in the pastry lid to allow steam to escape during baking.

12. Brush the pastry lid with the remaining egg white and sprinkle over the extra tablespoon of sugar. Place the dish on a roasting tray and bake for 45–50 minutes or until the pastry is a dark golden brown and the filling is bubbling.

13. Remove the pie from the oven and leave to cool slightly before serving. Once cold, you can store the pie in clingfilm for up to 24 hours, somewhere cool but not in the fridge.

14. Serve the pie with whipped cream.

Banana Cream Pie

SERVES 8–10

This is inspired by the banana cake at Momofuku in New York.
It's a show-stopping dessert to bring to any party.

INGREDIENTS

For the base

150g DARK CHOCOLATE, BROKEN INTO PIECES

100g UNSALTED BUTTER

250g DIGESTIVE BISCUITS

For the custard filling

275ml WHOLE MILK

300ml DOUBLE CREAM

250g CASTER SUGAR

1 TSP FINE SEA SALT

125g CORNFLOUR

1 VANILLA POD, SPLIT LENGTHWAYS

6 MEDIUM EGG YOLKS

8 X 1.6g PREMIUM-GRADE LEAVES OF GELATINE
(OR ENOUGH GELATINE TO SET 2 PINTS LIQUID)

1 TSP YELLOW FOOD COLOURING

For the topping

4 RIPE BANANAS

JUICE OF ¼ LEMON

500ml DOUBLE CREAM

50g CASTER SUGAR

METHOD

1. Line the base and sides of a 20–23cm round springform cake tin with parchment paper.

2. For the base, place the chocolate and butter in a medium heatproof bowl. Bring a small saucepan, a quarter-full of water, to a gentle simmer. Place the heatproof bowl on top, resting on the edge of the pan, so that no part of the bowl touches the water. Turn down the heat to a gentle simmer and leave until the butter and chocolate have completely melted, stirring now and again to mix. Remove the bowl from the pan and leave to cool slightly.

3. Blitz the biscuits in a food processor until they resemble breadcrumbs. Pour the cooled, melted chocolate mixture into the food processor and blend well.

4. Tip the crumb mixture into the cake tin and flatten with the back of a spoon. Place in the fridge to firm up while you make the custard filling.

5. For the custard filling, place the milk, cream, sugar, salt, cornflour and the seeds scraped out of the split vanilla pod in a medium saucepan. Mix, then whisk over a medium–low heat until thickened – about 8 minutes.

6. Remove the custard mixture from the heat and leave to cool slightly. Put the egg yolks in a mixing bowl, add a spoonful of the custard and mix well. Now pour the rest of the custard into the bowl, too, and stir thoroughly. Finally, pour the mixture back into the saucepan over a low heat, stirring for 3–4 minutes to cook the egg yolks gently. Remove from the heat and leave to cool for a few minutes.

7. Soak the gelatine in a bowl of cold water until soft, then squeeze out excess moisture and add to the warm custard. Mix well until the gelatine has dissolved. Stir in the food colouring.

8. To make the topping, slice the bananas and toss them in the lemon juice. Remove the cake tin from the fridge and arrange the sliced bananas over the biscuit base. Spoon over the custard and lay a sheet of clingfilm directly on the top to prevent a skin from forming.

9. Return the cake tin to the fridge and leave to set for at least 6–8 hours, ideally overnight.

10. To serve, whip the remaining cream and sugar, until stiff. Remove the clingfilm from the custard and spread the whipped cream over the top. Carefully remove the pie from the tin and cut into slices.

Knickerbocker Glory

SERVES 4

Before opening the first Byron, we used to borrow a friend's restaurant kitchen in the early hours to conduct endless menu tastings. It's on this basis that Tom believes he holds the world record for the number of Knickerbocker Glorys consumed before 7.30a.m. (four).

INGREDIENTS

For the poached strawberries

200g FRESH OR FROZEN STRAWBERRIES, HULLED

50g CASTER SUGAR

JUICE OF ¼ LEMON

For the rest of the dish

3 TBSP FLAKED ALMONDS

200ml DOUBLE CREAM

4 SCOOPS OF CHOCOLATE ICE CREAM (APPROX. 250g)

4 SCOOPS OF STRAWBERRY ICE CREAM (APPROX. 250g)

4 SCOOPS OF VANILLA ICE CREAM (APPROX. 250g)

QUICK CHOCOLATE SAUCE (SEE PAGE 169), WARMED SO THAT IT'S RUNNY

4 MARASCHINO CHERRIES

METHOD

1. For the poached strawberries, put all the ingredients in a small saucepan. Cook over a medium heat for about 4–5 minutes, stirring, until the sugar has dissolved and the strawberries have softened and released some of their juices. Remove from the heat and leave to cool.

2. For the rest of the dish, toast the flaked almonds in a small, hot frying pan over a medium heat for 6–7 minutes. Shake the pan occasionally and keep an eye on the almonds, removing them from the heat as soon as they are beautifully golden.

3. Just before you want to serve the dish, put the double cream in a mixing bowl and whip with an electric or balloon whisk until stiff peaks form.

4. Put a scoop of chocolate ice cream in the bottom of 4 sundae glasses and press down into the base. Top with a scoop of strawberry ice cream and then a spoonful of poached strawberries. Drizzle a spoonful of the strawberry juice over the top.

5. Top with a scoop of vanilla ice cream and press down slightly. Drizzle over a little Quick Chocolate Sauce to cover the vanilla ice cream.

6. Top with whipped cream, then a little more chocolate sauce. Sprinkle over the toasted almonds and garnish with a cherry.

Caramel & Honeycomb Sundae

SERVES 4

A satisfying, five-minute dessert. Tom's brother Robert swears by it.

INGREDIENTS

2 CRUNCHIE BARS OR OTHER CHOCOLATE-COATED HONEYCOMB BARS (80g IN TOTAL), FINELY CHOPPED

200g DULCE DE LECHE OR CARNATION CARAMEL

650g VANILLA ICE CREAM

METHOD

1. Separate the chopped Crunchie bars into 4 piles.

2. Put a spoonful of the dulce de leche in the bottom of each of 4 sundae glasses. Top with a small ball of ice cream, pushing down so there are no air bubbles between it and the dulce de leche.

3. Drizzle a little more of the dulce de leche around the insides of the sundae glasses, just above the ball of the vanilla ice cream. Put half of each pile of Crunchie pieces on top of the ice cream.

4. Top each glass with 3 more balls of ice cream.

5. Drizzle over the remaining dulce de leche, top with the remaining Crunchie pieces and serve with a long-handled spoon.

Oreo & Brownie Sundae

SERVES 4

Cookie-y, chocolatey and fun.
To make drizzling easier, pour the chocolate sauce into a squeezy bottle and warm it briefly in the microwave.

INGREDIENTS

250ml DOUBLE CREAM, OR 1 CAN OF AEROSOL WHIPPED CREAM IF YOU PREFER

2-3 PORTIONS OF CHOCOLATE BROWNIES (SEE PAGE 146)

12 OREO COOKIES

600g VANILLA ICE CREAM

QUICK CHOCOLATE SAUCE (SEE PAGE 169)

METHOD

1. Just before serving, pour the double cream into a medium mixing bowl and whip with an electric or balloon whisk until stiff peaks form.

2. Chop the Chocolate Brownies and 8 of the Oreo cookies into small chunks.

3. Put a ball of ice cream in the bottom of each of 4 sundae glasses. Press the ice cream down so that it completely covers the bottom.

4. Spoon a layer of Quick Chocolate Sauce over the ice cream, completely covering it. Sprinkle over half the brownie and Oreo cookie chunks.

5. Top with 2 more balls of ice cream. Divide the remaining brownie and Oreo chunks between the glasses.

6. Spoon or squirt some whipped cream into each glass and drizzle over the remaining chocolate sauce. Push a whole Oreo cookie into the side of each mound of cream and serve with a long-handled spoon.

Banana Split

With almonds for much-needed crunch, this is an ideal treat-pudding for kids, grown-ups, everyone.

INGREDIENTS

3 TBSP FLAKED ALMONDS

250ML DOUBLE CREAM

4 SCOOPS OF VANILLA ICE CREAM (APPROX. 200G)

4 SCOOPS OF CHOCOLATE ICE CREAM (APPROX. 200G)

4 SCOOPS OF STRAWBERRY ICE CREAM (APPROX. 200G)

4 BANANAS, PEELED AND SLICED IN HALF LENGTHWAYS

QUICK CHOCOLATE SAUCE (SEE PAGE 169), WARMED ENOUGH TO BE RUNNY

8 MARASCHINO CHERRIES

METHOD

1. Toast the flaked almonds in a small frying pan over a medium heat for 6–7 minutes. Shake the pan occasionally and keep an eye on the almonds, removing them from the heat as soon as they turn gold.

2. Just before you want to serve the dish, put the double cream in a mixing bowl and whip with an electric or balloon whip until stiff peaks form.

3. Put a scoop of each ice cream in a line along each of 4 oval dishes or banana split boats. Tuck a banana half on either side of the ice cream scoops, pushing them against the ice cream.

4. Drizzle over the Quick Chocolate Sauce. Divide the whipped cream between the dishes, adding dollops on top of each scoop of ice cream.

5. Sprinkle with the toasted almonds. Garnish with 2 maraschino cherries and serve.

Caramel & Honeycomb Blondie

MAKES 12–16, DEPENDING ON SIZE

A blondie is simply a white-chocolate brownie,
and this went down very well when we ran it as a special.

INGREDIENTS

4 MEDIUM EGGS

250g LIGHT BROWN SOFT SUGAR

1 TSP VANILLA EXTRACT

¼ TSP FINE SEA SALT

250g UNSALTED BUTTER, MELTED

130g PLAIN FLOUR

160g WHITE CHOCOLATE (OR CHIPS), CHOPPED

100g DULCE DE LECHE OR CARNATION CARAMEL

2 CRUNCHIE BARS OR OTHER CHOCOLATE-COATED HONEYCOMB BARS (80g IN TOTAL), CUT INTO 1cm CHUNKS

METHOD

1. Preheat the oven to 160°C (325°F). Line a 20–23cm square baking tin with parchment paper.

2. Place the eggs, sugar, vanilla and salt in a mixing bowl and beat with an electric or balloon whisk until the mixture is thick, pale, creamy and almost doubled in size. This could take up to 10 minutes, or longer with a balloon whisk.

3. Add the melted butter, beating as you pour. Now add the flour and beat until smooth.

4. Stir in the white chocolate, making sure it is evenly distributed.

5. Tip the mixture into the baking tin. Dot over the dulce de leche, spacing it evenly across the surface of the blondie, so that everyone's portion will include a bit of dulce de leche.

6. Sprinkle the chopped Crunchie bars evenly over the surface of the blondie, making sure you sprinkle right to the edges and into the corners, again so that everyone's portion will have some honeycomb in it.

7. Bake for 45–50 minutes or until just set. Once cooked, remove the tin from the oven and leave the blondie to cool.

8. Remove the blondies from the tin, trim the edges, cut into portions and serve. Any leftover blondies can be stored in an airtight container for up to 5 days.

163

Waffles with Blueberry Maple Butter

SERVES 4

Fred's girlfriend, previously a waffle-hater, was converted with this recipe.
They're delicious with Quick Chocolate Sauce (see page 169), or you can add blueberries to the batter.
Stir 50g fresh or frozen blueberries for every 125g mixture and cook as normal.

INGREDIENTS

250g PLAIN FLOUR

A PINCH OF FINE SEA SALT

25g CASTER SUGAR

¼ TSP DRIED ACTIVE YEAST

4 MEDIUM EGGS, SEPARATED

175ml WHOLE MILK

350ml DOUBLE CREAM

1 TBSP GOLDEN RUM

1 TSP VANILLA EXTRACT

For the blueberry maple butter

75ml PURE MAPLE SYRUP

150g UNSALTED BUTTER, CUBED

75g FRESH OR FROZEN BLUEBERRIES

METHOD

1. Sift the flour into a medium mixing bowl and add the salt, sugar and yeast. Mix until evenly distributed.

2. Whisk the egg yolks, milk, cream, rum and vanilla extract and then mix into the dry ingredients until everything is well combined.

3. In a separate, clean bowl, beat the egg whites with an electric or balloon whisk until stiff peaks form. Stir a spoonful of the whisked egg whites into the batter and mix with a large spoon until completely combined. Now gently fold the remaining whisked egg whites into the batter, until the egg whites are evenly incorporated.

4. Gently pour the mixture into a jug, for ease of pouring, cover and refrigerate for at least 1 hour, or up to 2 days. After this time the batter will look slightly frothy, with small bubbles forming at the surface.

5. Just before you cook your waffles, make the blueberry maple butter. Pour the maple syrup in a small saucepan and bring to a simmer. Reduce the heat to low and whisk in the butter, a little at a time, until completely melted. Add the blueberries and remove the pan from the heat. Keep warm while you cook the waffles.

6. To cook the waffles, heat a waffle machine/iron according to the manufacturer's instructions. Once hot, pour the batter in batches into the waffle machine; depending on the machine, the amount of batter will be somewhere between 125ml and 225ml – about a ladleful for standard-sized waffle machines. Cook according to the manufacturer's instructions until the waffles are golden and puffy. Repeat with the remaining batter.

7. Serve the waffles warm with the blueberry maple butter poured over the top.

Pancakes with Maple Syrup

SERVES 4

This is Fred's attempt to recreate the incredible pancakes that he and Tom enjoyed at Friend of a Farmer, a country-style American restaurant in New York. For blueberry pancakes, add a handful of fresh or frozen blueberries to the batter, stirring them through before you cook the pancakes.

INGREDIENTS

375g PLAIN FLOUR

1 TBSP BAKING POWDER

90g CASTER SUGAR

½ TSP FINE SEA SALT

375ml WHOLE MILK

3 MEDIUM EGGS, SEPARATED

70g UNSALTED BUTTER, MELTED AND
COOLED SLIGHTLY

1 TSP VANILLA EXTRACT

BUTTER OR VEGETABLE OIL, FOR COOKING

PURE MAPLE SYRUP, TO SERVE

METHOD

1. Sift the flour, baking powder, sugar and salt into a medium bowl and mix.

2. In a separate bowl, whisk the milk, egg yolks, melted butter and vanilla extract. Now pour this into the bowl of dry ingredients. Mix everything together well to form a smooth batter, but be careful not to over-mix, as this will make your pancakes heavy.

3. In a third bowl, beat the egg whites with an electric or balloon whisk until soft peaks form. Gently fold the whisked egg whites into the batter with a large spoon, being careful not to knock out the air.

4. Heat a large, non-stick frying pan over a medium heat. Add a tiny knob of butter or a splash of oil and rub around the pan with a piece of kitchen paper.

5. Add a small ladle of the batter to the pan to make a pancake about 6–8cm in diameter. Cook until small bubbles break the surface of the pancake and the underside is golden, then turn the pancake over with a fish slice or palette knife and cook for a further minute or until golden. Keep the cooked pancakes warm, wrapped in a clean tea towel or in a low oven while you cook the remaining batter.

6. Serve the pancakes warm with lots of maple syrup on the side.

Chocolate Chip Cookies

MAKES 20–24

Slightly crisp but with a chewy centre: a classic cookie.

INGREDIENTS

150g UNSALTED BUTTER, SOFTENED

350g LIGHT BROWN SOFT SUGAR

1 TSP VANILLA EXTRACT

1 WHOLE MEDIUM EGG, PLUS 1 YOLK

300g PLAIN FLOUR

½ TSP BAKING POWDER

A PINCH OF FINE SEA SALT

400g CHOCOLATE CHIPS (A MIXTURE OF DARK, MILK AND WHITE CHOCOLATE, IF POSSIBLE)

METHOD

1. Preheat the oven to 180°C (350°F).

2. In a large mixing bowl, cream the butter and sugar with an electric whisk or a wooden spoon. Now mix in the vanilla extract, the whole egg and the yolk.

3. Sift in the flour, baking powder and salt and mix together. Add the chocolate chips and mix again briefly until they are evenly distributed through the dough.

4. Break off pieces of cookie dough the size of golf balls and roll between your hands into neat balls. Arrange on 2 baking trays lined with parchment paper, spacing the balls apart to allow for spreading.

5. Bake for 12–15 minutes until golden. Remove from the oven (they will firm up once they begin cooling) and leave on the trays for a couple of minutes before transferring to a wire rack to cool.

6. Eat warm or leave to cool and store for up to 3 days in an airtight container.

No-Churn Easy Ice Cream

Our close friend and Byron devotee, Pooch, kindly gave us this great, simple recipe.
No ice-cream maker needed, no whipping with a fork and no repeated visits to the freezer.
Just blitz, freeze and eat. For more flavours, see the alternatives given below.

INGREDIENTS

600ml DOUBLE CREAM

200g CONDENSED MILK

2 TSP VANILLA EXTRACT, OR 1 VANILLA POD,
SEEDS ONLY

METHOD

1. Put all the ingredients in a large mixing bowl. Beat with an electric whisk until stiff peaks form.

2. Transfer to a suitable freezerproof container and freeze for at least 5 hours. The ice cream will keep for up to 3 months in the freezer.

ALTERNATIVE FLAVOURS

Chocolate: add 200g melted dark chocolate in Step 1.

Strawberry: add 300g hulled strawberries, blended until smooth, in Step 1.

Dulce de leche: swirl through a couple of tablespoons of dulce de leche at the end of Step 1.

Oreo: swirl through 1–2 handfuls of chopped Oreo cookies at the end of Step 1.

Quick Chocolate Sauce

SERVES 4

Knock this up in seconds to pimp up shop-bought ice cream.

INGREDIENTS

150G GOOD-QUALITY DARK CHOCOLATE, CHOPPED INTO SMALL PIECES

50G CASTER SUGAR

200ML DOUBLE CREAM

METHOD

1. Put the chocolate and sugar in a small heatproof bowl.

2. Pour the cream into a small saucepan over a medium heat. Heat to the point where small bubbles are breaking the surface, but the cream is nowhere near boiling.

3. Remove the pan from the heat and pour the cream straight into the bowl. Mix well with a spatula until the chocolate has completely melted and the sugar has dissolved. The sauce should be smooth and glossy.

4. Once cool, the sauce can be stored in an airtight container in the fridge for up to 6 days. If the sauce is cold and set, simply place in a heatproof bowl set over a pan of simmering water and heat until it is as runny as you need. Alternatively, give it a very brief blast in the microwave.

THE BYRON DECK

TALL TALE
Nº 10

I'd always been a poker fan, so when my friend Ben suggested that we give each of our restaurants an individual playing card as a business card (one side is the card, the other carries the address and phone number of the restaurant), it seemed like a no-brainer. After all, every restaurant is unique, but they all have something in common. They're all part of a pack.

One thing we didn't give much thought to in those very early days was what we'd do when we reached 52 - a complete deck. (No jokers, thanks - we've got enough of those on our hands already...) But nearly eight years later, that's exactly where we found ourselves.

All anyone seemed to want to know was what we'd do when we opened Byron no. 53. Happy Families? Tarot cards? Well, I've never been much of a fan of either of these. And the playing cards have become a big part of who we are. So we've launched into a new deck with a brand new design.

Turns out they're not much good for playing poker with; memorise which restaurant is which card and you can cheat very effectively. I guess you can't have everything.

Chocolate Chip Cookie Ice-Cream Sandwiches

MAKES 4

The man or woman who first took two cookies, placed a dollop of ice cream between them and ate them as a sandwich, may have been slightly bonkers. But it works exceptionally well.

INGREDIENTS

4 SCOOPS OF ICE CREAM, E.G. VANILLA, CHOCOLATE OR CARAMEL

8 CHOCOLATE CHIP COOKIES (SEE PAGE 167)

METHOD

1. Remove the ice cream from the freezer about 10 minutes before you want to use it.

2. Place 4 of the cookies upside down on a board or plate. Place a scoop of ice cream on each and top with the remaining cookies.

3. Press the sandwiches down slightly to squash and spread the ice cream to the edges. If you want a really neat ice-cream sandwich, then use a palette or table knife to skim around the edges of the ice cream and create a smooth surface.

4. Serve immediately.

CHAPTER 8

Drinks

The drinks in this chapter do different things. Homemade lemonade and iced tea refresh: there is nothing more cooling and delicious on a hot day. In summer, the kitchens sometimes knock up pitchers of minty, fruity iced tea for the staff to sip while working. The Bloody Caesar and the Bloody Bull will revive you like nothing else.

You may not have enjoyed a Shirley Temple or a Roy Rogers before. I believe they have been wrongly neglected in recent years.

Children love them. Finally, milkshakes – both hard and soft – offer a filling, almost dessert-like accompaniment to many of the dishes in this book.

Homemade Lemonade

SERVES 4

*To make sparkling lemonade, halve the amount of water you pour into the food processor,
then top with chilled sparkling water or soda water before serving.*

INGREDIENTS

6 UNWAXED LEMONS

100g CASTER SUGAR, PLUS EXTRA TO TASTE

METHOD

1. Grate the zest from 1 of the lemons and place in a food processor. Squeeze the juice from all the lemons into the food processor. Finally, add the flesh of half an unzested lemon.

2. Add the sugar and 100ml water. Blend to a purée.

3. Pour in 1 Litre chilled water and blend again until mixed. Taste and add a little more sugar, if necessary. Blend again if you added more sugar.

Depending on the size of your food processor, you may need to add the water in batches.

4. Strain the mixture through a fine sieve and into a jug. Discard the pulp. Store the lemonade, covered, in the fridge until completely cold.

5. Serve the chilled lemonade in glasses with plenty of ice.

Iced Tea

SERVES 4

*In the kitchens during the summer, the Byron teams often make pitchers of this to keep them cool but caffeinated –
very refreshing. If you prefer a less smoky flavour, then omit the Lapsang Souchong.*

INGREDIENTS

3 EARL GREY TEA BAGS

3 STANDARD (E.G. ENGLISH BREAKFAST) TEA BAGS

1 LAPSANG SOUCHONG TEA BAG

2 ORANGES, SLICED

1 LEMON, SLICED

5 SPRIGS OF MINT

75g CASTER SUGAR

METHOD

1. Place all the ingredients in a jug or large mixing bowl, squeezing the orange and lemon slices between your hands as you add them. Pour in 1.25 Litres boiling water and leave to steep for 10–20 minutes.

2. Pour the steeped mixture through a sieve and into another jug. Discard the contents of the sieve. Store the iced tea, covered, in the fridge until completely cold.

3. Serve the chilled ice tea in tall glasses with plenty of ice.

Bloody Caesar

MAKES 1 GLASS

The best way to banish a Sunday-morning hangover.
The secret here is to use Clamato, a Canadian tomato
juice flavoured with a little clam extract.
It is not fishy at all and tastes delicious.

50ML VODKA

175ML CLAMATO JUICE

JUICE OF ½ SMALL LEMON

½ TSP WORCESTERSHIRE SAUCE

¼ TSP TABASCO SAUCE, OR TO TASTE

¼ TSP CELERY SALT

SEA SALT AND FRESHLY GROUND BLACK PEPPER

CELERY STICK, TO SERVE

METHOD

1. Mix all the ingredients in a tall glass until combined.

2. Season with salt and pepper as necessary.

3. Serve with plenty of ice.

Bloody Bull

MAKES 1 GLASS

Tom became addicted to this hard man's
Bloody Mary at JG Melon in New York.
Beef stock is substituted for part of the tomato juice.
One for the stout of heart.

50ML VODKA

100ML CLAMATO JUICE

75ML CANNED BEEF CONSOMMÉ (IDEALLY CAMPBELL'S)

JUICE OF ½ SMALL LEMON

½ TSP WORCESTERSHIRE SAUCE

¼ TSP TABASCO SAUCE, OR TO TASTE

¼ TSP CELERY SALT

SEA SALT AND FRESHLY GROUND BLACK PEPPER

METHOD

1. Mix all the ingredients in a tall glass until combined.

2. Season with salt and pepper as necessary.

3. Serve with plenty of ice.

Shirley Temple

MAKES 1 GLASS

A fun "mocktail" to offer children at a drinks party, so they don't feel left out.
The story goes that the recipe was invented by a Beverly Hills bartender for the (then) child actress Shirley Temple.
Allegedly, she wasn't a fan, but we're sure your children will be.

INGREDIENTS

ICE CUBES

250ML SPARKLING LIME-LEMON DRINK, SUCH AS SPRITE

2 TSP GRENADINE SYRUP

2–3 MARASCHINO CHERRIES

METHOD

1. Half-fill a tall glass with ice. Add the sparkling-lime lemon drink.

2. Pour in the grenadine slowly to create a layered effect.

3. Serve with a couple of maraschino cherries as a garnish.

Roy Rogers

MAKES 1 GLASS

Named after the legendary American cowboy movie actor – though it's unclear why – this drink includes
grenadine and a maraschino cherry, for a fun alternative to a plain glass of cola.

INGREDIENTS

ICE CUBES

1 TBSP GRENADINE SYRUP

250ML FULL-FAT COLA

1 MARASCHINO CHERRY

METHOD

1. Half-fill a tall glass with ice. Add the grenadine, then pour in the cola.

2. Stir gently and serve with a maraschino cherry on top.

Vanilla Milkshake

MAKES 1 GLASS

INGREDIENTS

4 BIG SCOOPS OF VANILLA ICE CREAM (APPROX. 300g)

150ml MILK

METHOD

1. Using a stick blender, a blender or a food processor, blitz the ice cream and milk until smooth.

2. Serve immediately, in a large glass with a thick straw.

Strawberry Milkshake

MAKES 1 GLASS

INGREDIENTS

4 BIG SCOOPS OF STRAWBERRY ICE CREAM (APPROX. 300g)

150ml MILK

METHOD

1. Using a stick blender, a blender or a food processor, blitz the ice cream and milk until smooth.

2. Serve immediately, in a large glass with a thick straw.

Add 2 teaspoons malt powder to any of these shakes for a malt shake,

or add a shot of your favourite spirit to make a cheeky hard shake.

Chocolate Milkshake

MAKES 1 GLASS

INGREDIENTS

4 BIG SCOOPS OF CHOCOLATE ICE CREAM (APPROX. 300g)

150ml MILK

METHOD

1. Using a stick blender, a blender or a food processor, blitz the ice cream and milk until smooth.

2. Serve immediately, in a large glass with a thick straw.

Byron's Famous
Oreo Cookie Milkshake

MAKES 1 GLASS

*Simple but utterly delicious. It may be that the best part is at the end,
when you scoop up the bits of cookie that have collected at the bottom of the glass.*

INGREDIENTS

4 BIG SCOOPS OF VANILLA ICE CREAM (APPROX. 300G)

2 OREO COOKIES, BROKEN INTO PIECES

150ML MILK

METHOD

1. Using a stick blender, a blender or a food processor, blitz the ice cream, Oreo cookies and milk until smooth but with some specks of Oreo visible.

2. Serve straightaway in a large glass with a thick straw.

Banoffee Milkshake

MAKES 1 GLASS

As well as providing a subtle note of additional flavour, the banana improves the texture.

INGREDIENTS

4 BIG SCOOPS OF VANILLA ICE CREAM (APPROX. 300G)

150ML MILK

100G PEELED AND CHOPPED BANANA (APPROX. ½ BANANA)

1½ TBSP DULCE DE LECHE OR BUTTERSCOTCH SAUCE

METHOD

1. Using a stick blender, a blender or a food processor, blitz the ice cream, milk, banana and dulce de leche or butterscotch sauce until smooth.

2. Serve immediately, in a large glass with a thick straw.

INDEX

ACKNOWLEDGEMENTS

Tom and Fred would like to thank:

The Byron team – past and present – from the 14 who launched Kensington in 2007 to the 1,400 who work with us today.

Our extended family of designers and suppliers.

Céline Hughes and the whole team at Quadrille.

Veronique Baxter at David Higham Associates.

Cristina Fedi, our Head of Brand at Byron, for working tirelessly to ensure the Byron spirit shines through not just in this book but in everything we do.

Oliver Thring, Claire Strickett, Pooch Horsburgh and Michal Bielecki for invaluable help with words and recipes.

Richard and Linda Smith for constant unwavering support.

Flo, James, Perla, Alexander and Jess for honest feedback and keeping it fun.

Annabel, Rose, Johnny and Harry Byng – Byron's toughest critics and staunchest supporters.

ABOUT TOM & FRED

In 2007, frustrated at the lack of authentic US burgers in London, restaurateur Tom set up Byron opening its first restaurant on Kensington High Street.

Since then it has proved a huge hit amongst critics, foodies and customers, combining an obsession with delivering the perfect hamburger with stylish design, personable service and a hip brand.

Today, Byron has 60 individually designed restaurants and serves over 130,000 customers every week.

Fred is an experienced chef who shares Tom's passion for burgers and US food culture. After living in California for a year as a child, Fred was hooked on hamburgers from an early age. As a restaurant chef, he eschewed the lure of fine dining in favour of more comforting, satisfying dishes. He is in charge of the distinctive Byron menu.

Tom and Fred regularly travel to the US in search of new ideas and inspiration.

PUBLISHING DIRECTOR SARAH LAVELLE
CREATIVE DIRECTOR HELEN LEWIS
SENIOR EDITOR CÉLINE HUGHES
DESIGNER SAM MUIR
WWW.SAMUELMUIR.COM
DESIGN ASSISTANT EMILY LAPWORTH
PHOTOGRAPHERS MARTIN POOLE,
AMY CURRELL, ANDREW LEO
FOOD STYLISTS ROSIE REYNOLDS,
RUKMINI IYER
HOME ECONOMIST POOCH HORSBURGH
PROP STYLISTS RACHEL VERE,
ALEXANDER BREEZE
PRODUCTION STEPHEN LANG,
VINCENT SMITH

First published in 2016 by
Quadrille Publishing
Pentagon House
52–54 Southwark Street
London SE1 1UN
www.quadrille.co.uk

Quadrille is an imprint of Hardie Grant
www.hardiegrant.com.au

Reprinted in 2016
10 9 8 7 6 5 4 3 2